Lord, Save My Family

Other Books by Richard W. O'Ffill

Expect Great Things: How to Be a Happy, Growing Christian

If With All Your Heart: A God-Seeker's Guide to Effective Prayer

Lord, Keep Your Mansions—Just Save My Children

Standing Firm: A Practical Guide for Living in the Last Days

Transforming Prayer

GOD'S END-TIME MESSAGE FOR UNITY IN THE HOME

Lord, Save My Family

BEFORE IT'S TOO LATE

Richard W. O'Fill

Pacific Press® Publishing Association
Nampa, Idaho
Oshawa, Ontario, Canada
www.pacificpress.com

Copyright 2005 by Pacific Press® Publishing Association
Printed in the United States of America
All rights reserved

Book design by Dennis Ferree
Cover illustration Justinen Creative Group ©

Library of Congress Cataloging-in-Publication Data

O'Ffill, Richard, 1940–
Lord, save my family before it's too late : God's end-time message
for unity in the home / Richard W. O'Ffill.
p.cm.
ISBN 0-8163-2078-0
1. Family—Religious aspects—Christianity. I. Title

BT707.7.O35 2005
248.4'867–dc22   2005042990

For information on Richard O'Ffill's ministry,
please go to <www.revivalsermons.org>.

Additional copies of this book are available by calling toll free
1-800-765-6955 or visiting http://www.adventistbookcenter.com.

05 06 07 08 09 • 5 4 3 2 1

Dedication

This book is dedicated to my wife, Betty,
and to my children and grandchildren,
who together are my family.

"Behold, I will send you Elijah the prophet

before the coming of the great and dreadful day of the Lord:

And he shall turn the heart of the fathers to the children,

and the heart of the children to their fathers,

lest I come and smite the earth with a curse"

(Malachi 4:5, 6).

Table of Contents

CHAPTER

1

It's Never
Too Late

*"The difference between a house and a home is this: A house may fall down,
but a home is broken up."*—Elbert Hubbard (1856-1915)

I was sitting on the platform. It was nearly time for me to preach.
We'd sung the hymns and given our offering, and now someone was
telling the children's story. As I looked across the congregation, I realized that what we refer to as the church family is simply the sum of the
individual families that comprise the church. In that moment, the
thought flashed into my mind that the renewal, reformation, and revival that the church needs can happen only when these changes occur in our individual homes. How can the spiritual vitality of the church
amount to more than what its members bring to it? And how can
members bring more spiritual vitality to a church than they have at
home?

When God finished creating the world and all that was in it, He
established two institutions, the Sabbath and marriage. He blessed
and sanctified them. The one would unite us to Him, and the other
would be the very foundation of all that makes up communities,
cities, and nations—the family. No wonder the enemy has made it
his priority to destroy both institutions. As far as he is concerned,
obscuring and even nearly obliterating the Sabbath was relatively
easy. Destroying the home would prove to be more difficult. As his
satanic majesty begins his final moves just before the return of
our Lord in glory, his nefarious, two-pronged strategy is coming
together.

The devil's attempt to establish a false Sabbath we expected; but the success of his attack on the institution of marriage we couldn't have imagined in our worst nightmare. However, during the past few decades we have watched as the most sacred and holy of human relationships has been first trivialized and then corrupted. As it was in the days of Noah, when every thought was only evil continually, and as it was with the city of Sodom, so it is in these final days. Surely "it is time for Thee, Lord, to work: for they have made void thy law" (Psalm 119:126).

Throughout the history of this planet, just before each earth-shaking crisis that arose, God always sent a warning message to those who would hear. To us living at the end of the age, He has done the same. While in his final attack the devil aims to destroy the sacred institutions of the Sabbath and the home as God ordained them, we have the assurance that, as darkness shall cover the earth and gross darkness the people, the Lord shall arise upon us, and His glory shall be seen upon us (Isaiah 60:2). And though the enemy should come in like a flood, the Spirit of the Lord shall lift up a standard against him (Isaiah 59:19).

I am fascinated by the implications of Jesus' description of the last days, especially His words, "Because iniquity shall abound, the love of many shall wax cold" (Matthew 24:12). I have concluded that when love waxes cold, the family is affected first. This book stands in defense of the family. The promise and warning found in Malachi 4:5, 6 comprises its theme: "Behold, I will send you Elijah the prophet before the coming of the great and dreadful day of the Lord: And he shall turn the heart of the fathers to the children, and the heart of the children to their fathers, lest I come and smite the earth with a curse."

We see nations at war with one another, and we remark how much they need the gospel. Stories of looting and car bombs move us to give to missions so the gospel can change hearts and minds. So, yes, we know that the gospel changes lives. Then why do we seem to lock the gospel out of our homes? Where did we get the idea that Jesus' words "Love your enemies, bless them that curse you, do good to them that hate you, and pray for them which despitefully use you, and persecute you" (Matthew 5:44) apply to our treatment of everyone except our spouse?

Jesus commanded us to forgive not seven times but seventy times seven (see Matthew 18:22). We seem to have no problem with this as long as it does not refer to our attitude toward our parents. In short, we apply the command that we love our enemies to everyone except members of our own family. Experience has demonstrated that the most difficult place to be a Christian is at home. However, if we can't implement the principles of the gospel in our homes, we must question our ability to implement them anywhere.

On January 30, 2003, the space shuttle *Columbia* broke up on reentry into the earth's atmosphere. NASA's reaction was amazing. The administrators immediately suspended the space program. They directed a search that covered thousands of square miles and yielded more than eight thousand pieces of the broken spacecraft, which were then painstakingly reassembled. They pledged not to fly the shuttle again until they could ascertain exactly what happened that fateful day and take steps to prevent it from happening again. Homes throughout our society are crashing and burning. The marriage institution itself is at risk. Should we be any less diligent to discover causes and seek solutions?

In spite of the fact that the atmosphere of modern society is increasingly hostile to marriage and the family, there is hope for our families. But they will not survive by default. We must intentionally install a life-support system that will sustain us in the dark days before the dawn. That life-support system is the gospel as lived and taught by the Son of God Himself. If our families are to survive in these last days, we must allow the life of Jesus to come into our personal lives and from there to permeate the entire household.

Heart problems

The chapters that follow give a pastoral rather than a clinical perspective on the problems discussed and the solutions offered. Although I present some "how to's," the readers who will derive the greatest benefit are those who are willing to give their heart and life to Jesus and His Word. The problems that face us as individuals and as families are fundamentally heart problems that only being born again and accepting Jesus Christ as Savior and Lord will alleviate. You will notice the first chapters address issues that are not so much family issues as personal issues. Change in the family comes only one heart at a time.

Perhaps you tend to think that what you are reading applies to everyone else in the family except yourself. The principles enunciated in this book are no respecter of persons. They are for everyone in the family, including the reader.

Perhaps you haven't had a good track record in family relationships. You may be dealing with divorce and alienation. If this is your situation, you need not be disheartened. Although we cannot live our lives over again, by God's grace we can always get a new start. A recurring theme throughout the pages of this book is that, no matter where we come from or where we are now, the gospel of Jesus Christ will help us experience a new beginning.

Perhaps members of your family make no profession of religion and even act with a studied hostility to spiritual values. Don't worry; this book is for you as well. It will challenge you to consider the possibility that Jesus may use your changed heart to reach the hearts of your family.

The quality of intelligence gathered may determine whether a war is won or lost. Such was the case before the invasion of Normandy, which was the turning point in World War II. The Allies put together an elaborate plan to attack the Axis powers with what history would record as the largest invasion fleet ever assembled. There would be five thousand ships, eleven thousand planes, and 150,000 troops. The code name for the plan was Operation Overlord.

The victory won that day on the beaches of France was due to the valor of those who landed on those beaches, on the blood shed by the thousands who were killed and wounded. But the enemy could have repulsed the attack and prolonged the war had it not been for an elaborate lie.

To deceive the enemy and divert attention away from the actual invasion, the Allies formulated a deception with the code name Fortitude. The idea was to make it appear as though they were planning to focus the invasion on the Point de'Calais. To accomplish this, they established a paper army (the "First United States Army Group") that supposedly was comprised of a million men and was under the command of General George S. Patton. Its armor included fake tanks and trucks made of plywood and inflatable rubber, which, when seen by the enemy from the air, appeared to be the real thing. The enemy fell for the ruse, and what resulted on June 6, 1944, is a matter of history. The army of the Allies breached the enemy's heavily fortified defenses, and on May 7, 1945, Germany surrendered.

The devil also has a program of misinformation as he seeks to invade our souls and our families. During those critical days of World War II, Winston Churchill said that truth is so precious that it must be accompanied by a bodyguard of lies. It occurs to me that our enemy has given that saying a twist. He wraps his deceptions in a thin skin of truth. He knocks on the doors of our homes, misrepresenting himself as a friend of the family and as a bearer of gifts.

It is my prayer that this book will help to expose some of the misinformation that seems to be entering like a flood. Let's stop doing business as usual and put some of the pieces together. Using Bible principles, let's try to discover what is going wrong and how it can be fixed. Who knows but that this book may serve as a catalyst to bring revival, renewal, and reformation to your family—beginning with you.

As you read, when ideas pop into your mind as to how to make the gospel real in your home, I hope you will jot them down. Financial counselors suggest that when people have incurred a number of debts, they should begin the process of paying them off by paying first the ones with the lower balances. Similarly, I suggest that you start implementing at once those suggestions that are the most obvious and over which you have the most influence. Remember, it has taken time to get into the problems we have; getting out will take time too.

Each subsequent chapter ends with Points to Ponder. These points sum up the main thrust of the chapter. Each chapter also contains a Homework Assignment. You don't have to do exactly what is being suggested, but do something!

A Prayer for God's Blessing

Dear Heavenly Father,

You are the Father of all the families on earth. You established marriage and gave the first couple the ability to procreate, and You encouraged them to do so. Now, at the end of the age, the devil seems to have completely surrounded us. In many instances, he has overrun our defenses. Thank You, Lord, that in this dark time You have promised to save our homes with a special message that would turn our hearts to You and to each other.

May the Holy Spirit use this book to bring revival, renewal, and reformation into my home. And Father, give me the strength and patience to cooperate with You as You do this.

Amen.

CHAPTER
2

We Pack
Our Own Lunch

"Insanity is doing the same thing over and over and expecting different results."–Albert Einstein

It was twelve noon at the factory. The whistle blew, and the workers streamed out for lunch break. This particular day, two men found themselves sitting next to each other on a metal bench. One of the men was a big, tough-looking guy. The other, we would have to say, was just regular-size. They didn't know each other, and without even acknowledging each other's presence, they opened their lunch pails.

The big guy removed a waxed-paper-wrapped sandwich and lifted the edge of one of the pieces of bread to see what kind of filling it had. Talking more to himself than to the man next to him, he muttered. "Oh no! It's a peanut-butter sandwich." The other man pretended not to hear and nothing more was said.

The next day, lunchtime found the same two men sitting side by side again. The big man opened his lunch pail, unwrapped a sandwich, and lifted a corner of the bread to see what kind of sandwich it was. It was evident he was unhappy with what he discovered, for he said more loudly than the previous day, "Oh no! It's a peanut-butter sandwich!"

The third day presented nearly the same scenario. This time, however, when the big fellow discovered he'd gotten a peanut-butter sandwich again, he went into a rage.

The regular-size man could resist no longer. "Buddy," he said respectfully, "I notice you don't like peanut-butter sandwiches. Why don't you ask your wife to fix you something else?"

At that, the big man turned, stuck his fist in the other man's face, and said, "Shut your mouth! I pack my own lunch."

It's true. We all pack our own lunch. Someone has said we make our own bedlam, and we have to sleep in it. You see, life is a process of cause and effect. Nothing happens just by chance. Natural laws and principles control everything about our existence. We seem to understand this concept better when it plays out in the physical sciences. Let me explain. I believe it is safe to say that no one really invents anything. People simply discover the principles that are involved in the particular effect they are trying to produce, and then they manufacture the components that are consistent with those principles and put them together. Sound complicated? Well, it really isn't. Put simply, if we match the right causes, we will get the effects we want.

I think of this principle sometimes when I'm flying. An airplane must be designed consistent with the principles of aerodynamics or it won't fly. And the pilot must control the plane in a manner consistent with the same principles. He can't make up his own rules about how he'll fly. He can decide only whether or not he will fly. If he doesn't obey the laws of flight, he simply will not get off the ground.

Follow this thought: Nothing happens by chance or even by accident. What we call accidents are actually the results of causes that we didn't foresee or that we didn't even want to come together. We might call them accidents, but they're the result of definite causes. The world in which we live is predictable. The Bible puts it this way: "Be not deceived; God is not mocked: for whatsoever a man soweth, that shall he also reap" (Galatians 6:7). The apostle James illustrated the same principle: "Doth a fountain send forth at the same place sweet water and bitter? Can the fig tree, my brethren, bear olive berries? either a vine, figs? so can no fountain both yield salt water and fresh" (James 3:11, 12). And Jesus asked, "Do men gather grapes of thorns, or figs of thistles?" (Matthew 7:16).

The Christian life and, by extension, the Christian home are also subject to the law of cause and effect. A person who wants to make a cake must bring together the right ingredients and bake them at the right temperature for a specific amount of time. Likewise, if our homes are to be healthy physically, emotionally, and spiritually, we must bring together the ingredients that will produce the results we desire.

If indeed a happy home is no accident, neither is an unhappy home. If our homes are less than a little heaven on earth (the *effect*), perhaps we're not employing the right *causes*. Albert Einstein defined insanity as doing the same thing over and over and expecting different results. Could it be that some of us are sowing the same bad seeds and applying the same faulty ingredients in our families but expecting different and better results?

Forget the do's and don'ts?

There was a time when being a member of a conservative denomination meant that one was not to drink alcohol, smoke, go to the theater, or dance. Women were to dress modestly, and jewelry was not allowed. These standards served to give a certain structure to the church, society, and the Christian home. Now, however, these types of standards are largely a thing of the past, and many consider them to be legalism. The current wisdom has it that the Christian home shouldn't be a place where do's and don'ts are emphasized—rather, they say, Christianity is all about relationships.

Looking back across the years, I would have to agree that in the past we were indeed big into do's and don'ts. In fact, we were bigger into don'ts than into do's. But if life is indeed a product of cause and effect, is it possible to separate do's and don'ts from relationships? Are the two concepts adversarial, or are they, in fact, complementary?

Let's use as a practical illustration the relationship between husband and wife. After more than forty years of marriage, I feel I can speak with some authority. I have discovered that I nurture my relationship with my wife by the way I treat her—in plain language, by the things I do and don't do. I can say, "I love you, I love you, I love you" (and we should say these words often to each other), but if I don't back up these words with a little action (helping around the house, taking her out, buying her flowers), my professions of love won't be very convincing.

The principle of cause and effect has a negative side also. Thoughtlessness, rudeness, and disrespect can cause some pretty negative effects. All this boils down to the fact that what I do or don't do greatly affects my relationship with my wife. Somewhere along the way, however, we've picked up the idea that what we put into something doesn't necessarily have a bearing on what we get out of it—this, in spite of learning the cardinal rule of computers: "garbage in, garbage out."

The book of Proverbs can often be difficult to follow, because it seems to have been written mostly in sound bites. Rarely does a thought go from one verse to another. But Proverbs has probably the richest concentration of the principles of cause and effect in all of Scripture. Together, its verses comprise a huge list of do's and don'ts. Fortunately, proverbs are likelihoods, not irrevocable promises. Nevertheless, the basic concept is that if you want a certain effect to happen, you should do such-and-such. And if you don't want some other effect to happen, then you should avoid doing such-and-such. Life is certainly about relationships, and relationships are built up or broken down by do's and don'ts—the causes that inevitably result in effects.

In the contemporary culture, powerful forces exist whose effects are to greatly weaken, if not destroy, the home as we have known it. If we desire to establish a Christian home, we must be proactive and make intentional, well-informed decisions as to what we will include and what we will exclude from home life.

My wife and I live in Central Florida. During the summer months, we often have torrential rains in the afternoon. Usually they come and go quickly, but sometimes several inches of rain may fall in these showers. If the roof has a leak, in time the rain will find it—even if it's just a hairline crack. A small leak may not at first affect what lies beneath it, but it will eventually cause the roof sheeting to deteriorate. It may go unnoticed for several years, but when the homeowners finally discover it, they may have to repair a lot of damage.

Like a roof, our marriages can have a small leak or flaw that we don't detect until something begins to deteriorate. The problem is that we can repair rotten roof sheeting more easily than we can repair a rotten marriage.

There was a time when a family could survive despite bad relationships. The culture, the church, and even the extended family could hold things together. Those days seem to have passed. Moreover, it used to be that church people didn't seem to have the same kinds of problems as the unchurched. This, too, has changed. Increasingly, we're allowing the forces of contemporary culture to shape not only our worldview but also our way of life. Christian homes are now, as it were, taking direct hits, and unless we take steps to protect our marriage, we can easily become just another statistic. Whether by neglect or intentionally, we are in many instances employing causes that can have only one effect—the breakdown of the family as God meant for it to be. Could it be that we are collectively and as individuals flirting with insanity—doing the same things but expecting different results?

In times past, there was a sense of urgency to life, a raison d'être. But life has become casual and haphazard. Someone has suggested that perhaps the trouble is that families are no longer preparing for the coming of Jesus.

Tragically, the verses in 2 Timothy 3:1-5 describe what is happening in many Christian families now:

> This know also, that in the last days perilous times shall come. For men shall be lovers of their own selves, covetous, boasters, proud, blasphemers, disobedient to parents, unthankful, unholy, without natural affection, trucebreakers, false accusers, incontinent, fierce, despisers of those that are good, traitors, heady, highminded, lovers of pleasure more than lovers of God; having a form of godliness, but denying the power thereof.

This condition is not a result of chance or bad luck. Nothing in this world happens by chance. We pack our own lunch. Could the condition of many Christian families be due to the fact that they no longer consider relevant the command, "Love not the world, neither the things that are in the world. If any man love the world, the love of the Father is not in him" (1 John 2:15)?

Close the doors

The story of Old Testament Israel is a narrative of what happens when God's people became involved in the cultures of the unbelieving nations around them. They paid an awful price. Unless we learn the lesson, we will pay as well. In fact, Christian families of the twenty-first century are already paying a great price. We've opened our homes to the enemy of our souls, and he's doing great damage. As darkness covers the earth and gross darkness the people (Isaiah 60:2), we must immediately take steps to close the doors of our homes to anything and everything that is incompatible with the holy life God has commanded us to live. We must be intentional and diligent to allow into our homes only those things that will serve to build up the kingdom of God. It is a matter of cause and effect.

I invite you right now to do an inventory of your personal and family life. What are your family goals? Who are your role models? Are you allowing influences into your home that will result in heartache?

Some years ago, a family who served with us in South America dropped by our house to spend the night. This family enjoys pets, including snakes and lizards. They were on vacation at the time and were excited that along the way they had been able to capture a particular variety of snake they had always wanted. They were keeping the snake in an aquarium with a lid, and they asked if they could bring the aquarium into the house for the night. I told them they could, and we put the aquarium downstairs in the utility room.

The next morning the family gathered their things together, including the aquarium. Nothing was missing . . . except the snake, which somehow had escaped into the house during the night. And so our old friends left us a unique hostess gift—a snake loose in the house. Reading this may make you laugh, but to me it wasn't funny.

The snake eluded us for several months. One day I was making repairs and needed to use the electric skill saw. I picked it up and was about to turn it on when I discovered the snake tightly curled up in the metal shield that covers the blade. I put the saw down very quickly. Now, how was I to get him out? The answer came to me. I put the saw in the sunshine, it became hot, and the snake crawled away never to be seen again.

I share this experience because it reminds me that although we wouldn't do it on purpose, some of us have let snakes loose in our homes. Not the harmless, garden variety of snake, but the kind whose bite can cheapen family relationships and even paralyze spiritual growth. The negative things we experience in our homes may be an accident, but they are not accidental. We simply are reaping what we have sown. It is the law of cause and effect.

If our family life isn't turning out as we hoped, then we need to discover how we may be contributing to the results that we don't want. In most cases, if we're honest with ourselves, we don't need to have someone tell us what we are doing that we shouldn't. The truth is, we usually know better, even though, for the time being, the specifics may be lost in the muddle of life. The devil is dishing out a sweet syrup that tastes good. But if we consume what he's giving us, it will prove fatal to our most precious relationships.

The message that prepares us for the coming of Jesus also heals our homes. But it is one we must find in Scripture and not in our culture. We must, by the power of the Holy Spirit, implement this message in our homes while there is still time.

The next chapter points out that how we define a problem will determine what we do about it. Please take a moment now to review the Points to Ponder and then do the Homework Assignment.

Points to Ponder
1. Nothing happens by chance.
2. Not understanding or complying with do's and don'ts can make or break a relationship.
3. The book of Proverbs is a sound-bite approach to the do's and don'ts of living.
4. Though we may not have ordered our life circumstances, we are responsible for what we do with our life. Someone has said that life is 10 percent what happens to us and 90 percent how we respond.
5. Negative relationships in the home are increasingly the result of buying into current group thinking rather than the principles enunciated in the Word of God.

Homework Assignment
1. Identify two positive factors that seem to be working in your home. Determine what it is that makes these positive factors successful.
2. Identify two things that are happening in your family that you wish were not. Analyze and list the probable causes. Remember, nothing happens by chance. Life is about causes and effects.

CHAPTER 3

A Rose by Any Other Name Is Still a Rose

*"If we say we have no sin, we deceive ourselves,
and the truth is not in us."*—the apostle John

A snail was crossing the road one day and was run over by a turtle. Someone called 911, an ambulance came, and the snail was taken to the emergency room. When it regained consciousness, the doctor asked what happened. The snail replied weakly, "I don't remember—it all happened so fast!"

So much of life is a matter of perspective. It is important that we try to see what is happening from God's point of view. Doing otherwise might lead us to think that things have always been the way they are now in our society.

Once, sin was sin and it seemed to be everywhere, given how often people referenced it. By contrast, these days we might conclude that the world must be getting better and better, because hardly anyone talks about sin any more. Has sin disappeared? The word *sin* used to be a proud word. It was a strong, ominous, and serious word. It named a concept that figured prominently in every civilized human being's life plan and lifestyle. It was something to be feared and avoided at all costs.

Some years ago, Dr. Karl Menninger wrote a book with a provocative title: *Whatever Became of Sin?* In the book, he argued that a particular act—say, committing adultery—was, in the days when religion was a rule of life, considered to be sin. The state governments carried things a step further and made adultery a crime, with penalties for violators. But as time passed and the church lost influence in the lives of the citizenry, the state decriminalized adultery. Now, what once had been a sin and later an act prohibited by law has become acceptable behavior. It no longer carries a stigma. In fact, the act is now rarely called adultery. It is simply referred to as an "affair."

But there is more. Increasingly, behaviors that people once considered sins are now viewed as illnesses. It is not uncommon, when someone has committed a horrible deed and the story is recounted, to hear "Tisk, tisk, tisk" and then "Sick, sick, sick." The important question no longer is whether people have actually committed the crimes of which they are accused. Rather, it is whether they were responsible at the time. Their lawyers try to convince the jury that the accused are sick. When that has been proven, they're seen as not responsible for what they've done and consequently, innocent of the charge.

Or, alternatively, when someone goes amuck, modern society often sees the cause to be unfavorable circumstances. People may get the credit for their successes, but their mistakes will likely be attributed to drug addiction, ignorance, bad genes, malfunctioning neurotransmitters, poverty, mental illness, racism, or sexism—anything but the perpetrators themselves. The immaturity and evasiveness of this perspective reminds me of the day I asked my little son Richard to pick up his toys. His reply? "I can't—my hands are too little."

When things go wrong, the modus operandi—from the time of our first parents until now—has been to blame something or someone else. When God asked Adam what he had done, Adam blamed someone else—his wife. When God asked Eve what she had done, she blamed something else—the serpent. Generally, people who have been accused of something deny their guilt. Even if caught with their hand in the cookie jar, offenders try to give some reason as to why they did it, or better yet, to suggest that someone else made them do it.

It would be impossible to play a game of tennis if players who hit the ball out of the court were exempted from penalty if they could convince the umpire that it was not what they intended to do. Yet increasingly, we don't see ourselves as responsible, moral agents but rather as victims of our bodily, familial, or societal dysfunctions. It is as if we somehow consider ourselves impaired and thus can excuse our "mistakes" because either we didn't mean to do what we did or we couldn't help doing it.

However, from the very beginning, God has related to those whom He created in His own image as responsible for their actions. The poet John Milton wrote (speaking from God's perspective):

> I formed them free, and free they must remain
> Till they enthrall themselves: I else must change
> Their nature, and revoke the high decree
> Unchangeable, eternal, which ordained
> Their freedom; they themselves ordained their fall.
> —*Paradise Lost,* book 3, lines 1124–1128

What we need

The plan of salvation can work in our life only when we accept the principle of personal responsibility. Throughout Scripture, from the expulsion from the Garden all the way to the final destruction of the wicked, the message is loud and clear. God treats human beings as free moral agents and holds them responsible for their actions. The punishment of the unrepentant and the forgiveness of the repentant imply personal responsibility.

Can you think of anyone in Scripture who committed sin yet wasn't considered to be responsible for the act? Cain, the first murderer, might have argued that Abel was always putting him down and what he did was the result of his low self-esteem. Moses might have argued that he disobeyed God because the people's continual complaining and demands had placed him under inordinate stress. Yet God held these men and others responsible for what they did. Although Jesus is merciful and could say to the woman caught in adultery simply, "Don't do that anymore," nothing in Scripture implies that He absolved her of her responsibility.

From Genesis to Revelation, the Holy Spirit calls people to repent, and the concept of repentance is based on personal responsibility. If we are not responsible for what we do, then God's interactions with humankind throughout history amount only to incoherent acts of savage punishment and capricious reward. Our continued insistence that mitigating circumstances in life somehow absolve us of responsibility for what we do isn't eliminating our familial and societal problems. On the contrary, it is multiplying the negative effects.

Some time ago, I was to speak at a revival meeting being conducted in Okeechobee, Florida. Having been there once before, I remembered that it was several hours from where I live in Orlando, and I knew the general direction. I thought I knew the route, so without consulting a map, I took off down the road on a trip I figured would take about two hours.

After an hour and a half of driving, I became a little concerned. Where were the signs for Okeechobee? The scenery had changed from dry pastureland to swampy grassland and began to look for all the world like the Everglades. At that point, I stopped at the first convenience store I came to and asked the cashier when I was going to get to Okeechobee. "Never," he replied. "You're on the road to Miami."

I suppose I could have taken his reply as an insult or a putdown or, at the very least, damaging to my self-esteem. But it was none of these. He was actually doing me a favor. The choice as to how I was going to react to his answer was mine.

Although the result of my choice of roads was not what I intended, I wasn't going to get where I wanted to go if I kept going the way I was headed. The decision for me at that moment was not how or why I had taken the wrong road but what I was going to do about it.

Undoubtedly, ignorance, poverty, racism, sexism, bad genes, dangerous drugs, child abuse, sex abuse, and other factors affect our lives, sometimes severely. Though Scripture doesn't hold the fact that we've been victims of these things against us, neither does it absolve us of responsibility for what we do as a result. God doesn't hold us responsible for what we do so He can punish us. Rather, He holds us responsible for our actions so He can save us.

Determinism is a basic premise of the father of modern psychotherapy, Sigmund Freud. In lay language, determinism declares that what we are today was determined early in our life, and so is our future; there is little possibility for change. However, Christianity says that although there can be no doubt that I am a product of all my yesterdays, as I accept responsibility for what I am, Christ offers hope for a changed tomorrow. While the message of contemporary culture is that we are what we are and we might as well make the best of it, the message of the gospel is that "if we confess our sins, He is faithful and just to forgive us our sins and to cleanse us from all unrighteousness" (1 John 1:9). The message is that in Jesus, it is never too late to get a new start.

Some teach that our environment—especially that which our parents provided—is to blame for our troubles. The Bible does recognize that we may have come from dysfunctional homes. However, notice what it says in Ezekiel 18:20-22, 26-28, 30:

> The soul that sinneth, it shall die. The son shall not bear the iniquity of the father, neither shall the father bear the iniquity of the son: the righteousness of the righteous shall be upon him, and the wickedness of the wicked shall be upon him. But if the wicked will turn from all his sins that he hath committed, and keep all my statutes, and do that which is lawful and right, he shall surely live, he shall not die. All his transgressions that he hath committed, they shall not be mentioned unto him: in his righteousness that he hath done he shall live.
> . . .
> When a righteous man turneth away from his righteousness, and committeth iniquity, and dieth in them; for his iniquity that he hath done shall he die. Again, when the wicked man turneth away from his wickedness that he hath committed, and doeth that which is lawful and right, he shall save his soul alive. Because he considereth, and turneth away from all his transgressions that he hath committed, he shall surely live, he shall not die. . . . Therefore I will judge you, O house of Israel, every one according to his ways, saith the Lord God.

The message of these verses is unequivocal; God holds us and not our parents accountable for our actions. But He has promised that if we will take ownership of who we are and admit that what we are is not what He wants us to be, and if we are willing to let Him change us, He will give us a new heart.

The diagnosis

Whatever happened to sin? If we see our personal and family problems as only psychological, then we may decide that the solution is to make an appointment to see a counselor or a medical doctor. But when we see that our problems stem first from sin in our own hearts, then we will pray the prayer of David:

> Have mercy upon me, O God, according to Thy lovingkindness: according unto the multitude of Thy tender mercies blot out my transgressions. Wash me thoroughly from mine iniquity, and cleanse me from my sin. . . .
>
> Purge me with hyssop, and I shall be clean: wash me, and I shall be whiter than snow. Make me to hear joy and gladness; that the bones which Thou hast broken may rejoice. Hide Thy face from my sins, and blot out all mine iniquities.
>
> Create in me a clean heart, O God; and renew a right spirit within me (Psalm 51:1, 2, 7-10).

A rose by any other name is still a rose. Call it whatever we want, sin by any other name is still sin. Scripture identifies sin as the missing of the mark *(Greek harmartia)*. It is the crossing or transgressing of a line *(parabasis);* disobedience to a voice *(parakouō);* falling where one should have stood upright *(paraptōma);* ignorance of what one ought to have known *(agnoēma);* diminishing of that which should have been rendered in full measure *(hēttēma);* or the breaking of a law *(anomia or paranomia).*

Perhaps I should explain why, in a book entitled *Lord, Save My Family Before It's Too Late,* I would early on discuss sin—a subject that would seem to fit better in a book about theology. I have done this because I believe we can hope to heal our families only when we understand that the present condition in many of our homes is a result of what the Word of God calls sin. To acknowledge that we are missing the mark is not demeaning. Rather, it is the condition that we must meet before the restoration we so badly need will come into our homes (1 John 1:9).

How we diagnose a problem determines what we will do about it. Jesus came to save sinners. If we buy into the perspective of contemporary society, we may very well continue to rationalize and make excuses. Elijah called Israel to turn away from the ideologies of their time and return to God and to His Word. That message was right for the families represented on Mount Carmel, and it is right—yea, mandatory—for families today.

Points to Ponder
1. God has predicated the plan of salvation on personal accountability.
2. God doesn't hold us responsible for the choices we make in order to punish us but so that He can save us.
3. We place our families and ourselves in danger when we allow contemporary culture to set our standards of faith and morals.
4. How we diagnose a problem will determine the steps we take to solve it.
5. Undoubtedly, my yesterdays brought me to where I am today. But in Christ, I always have reason to hope for a new tomorrow.

Homework Assignment
1. Identify several areas in the life of your immediate family that are troublesome.
2. Find a Bible text that specifically addresses what you need to do in each instance.

CHAPTER
4

Mirror, Mirror on the Wall

"Reflection is the beginning of wisdom."
—Mark Twain (1856–1910)

I was talking with a young wife who also happened to be a mother and a businesswoman. She told me that so many things were going on in her life that she was nearly beside herself. Haven't we all had moments when we felt like a juggler with too many balls in the air and some of them made of glass? Eventually we reach the point where we just want to say, "Stop the world, I want to get off." But we can't get off, so we hold on for dear life.

It shouldn't come as a surprise that one of the devil's strategies at the end time is to so overload the circuits that the lines carrying the current of our lives begin to heat up. In the electrical systems in our houses, if something begins to overheat, the circuit breaker will cut off the current. But when it comes to our lives, we often aren't so lucky. Sometimes the important things that make up our lives catch fire and become permanently damaged.

As I pointed out in the last chapter, sometimes when we're dealing with our problems, we try to blame others. If that doesn't work, we simply say we couldn't help ourselves due to the damage we've sustained from dangerous drugs, sex abuse, ignorance, bad genes, malfunctioning neurotransmitters, poverty, mental illness, racism, or sexism. I'm not making light of serious things. I believe these things do real damage to our lives and our homes. However, many believe that people who have suffered any one of these tragedies are permanently ruined; if not spiritually, at least emotionally. The good news is that even though the things that have happened to us have deeply affected us, they need not incapacitate us or even hold us back.

On a radio talk show that I host, I once interviewed the director of Disabled Ministries in the conference where I worked. She developed rheumatoid arthritis when she was twelve years old, and the disease severely affected her arms and legs. She has spent most of her life in a wheelchair. During the interview, I asked her what it was like to be confined to her chair.

"Confined!" she exclaimed. Then she said something I have never forgotten. "The wheelchair is not confining, it is liberating."

Her reply brought tears to my eyes. And it has helped me better understand the meaning of the gospel. In this life at least, we can't expect the gospel to do away completely with the crippling effect that sin has had on us. But, praise God, the gracious plan of salvation liberates us, enabling us to get on with this life until the time comes when God will wipe away all tears from our eyes, and this vale of sorrow will be no more.

However, our lives are not solely the result of what others have done to us. We ourselves have built-in liabilities that, even if we were in a heavenly environment with angels for companions, would surely bring about our ruin. The Bible teaches that there is something sinister embedded in our very being. Consider this text: "The heart is deceitful above all things, and desperately wicked: who can know it?" (Jeremiah 17:9). And this one: "Out of the heart proceed evil thoughts, murders, adulteries, fornications, thefts, false witness, blasphemies" (Matthew 15:19).

Because human nature is intrinsically sinful, we can't say that a bad environment makes us bad. Rather, it merely brings out the bad that is already in us. I am reminded of what David said: "Behold, I was shapen in iniquity; and in sin did my mother conceive me" (Psalm 51:5).

Sometimes after I've preached, people will say to me, "I wish so-and-so had been here to hear that." I'm left to wonder if they meant that to be a compliment or if they felt that the sermon didn't apply to them and that I was wasting my time preaching to people who didn't need it. How do *you* listen to a sermon? Do you apply the lessons to your own life? Once we understand our own spiritual need, the world gets bigger, not smaller. Our outlook grows from "them" to "us." In terms of spiritual need, we must always keep ourselves in the loop.

This concept is important in the context of the family. If the atmosphere in our homes is to change, it will happen one person at a time. And for the purposes of this book, dear reader, it seems that person might as well be me—and you. This is not to infer that all the troubles in the home are my fault, or yours. Rather, a new start ought logically to begin with the person who wakes up to the need first, and in this case, that's you and I.

We need to remind ourselves every day that life is 10 percent what happens to us and 90 percent how we react. That's another way of saying that we can't keep the birds from flying over our heads, but we can keep them from nesting in our hair.

The Bible continually challenges us to look to what kind of people we ourselves are. Three texts immediately come to mind, one in the Old Testament and two in the New:

- Take heed to thyself, and keep thy soul diligently, lest thou forget the things which thine eyes have seen, and lest they depart from thy heart all the days of thy life (Deuteronomy 4:9).
- Let a man examine himself (1 Corinthians 11:28).
- Examine yourselves, whether ye be in the faith (2 Corinthians 13:5).

Someone may interpret this as being self-centered. But Scripture wouldn't be calling on us to do something that's self-centered.

Introspection

On studying the lives of outstanding men and women of God, we find that most had an on-going commitment to introspection. At first glance, looking at one's self may appear to involve a conflict of interest, because we tend to view ourselves in the best light and to "scapegoat" our faults on to someone or something else. But by bringing God into the exercise, we can keep this from happening. David prayed,

"Search me, O God, and know my heart: try me, and know my thoughts: and see if there be any wicked way in me" (Psalm 139:23, 24), and, "Examine me, O Lord, and prove me; try my reins and my heart" (Psalm 26:2).

Although I was raised on the King James Version of the Bible, the use of the word *reins* in that last text really stumped me, so I looked it up in a Hebrew lexicon. The word translated "reins" is the Hebrew word *kilyah*. Now, hold on to your chair: *kilyah* means "kidneys." (And I thought I had trouble with the word *reins!*) But then I found that the Hebrew people considered the kidneys to be the seat of emotion and affection. We have a couple expressions that use body parts similarly. We say, "My heart just wasn't in it," and, "I couldn't stomach what she was saying."

In other words, David was praying, "Lord, test me; check out everything about me." When God answers that prayer for us and checks us out, more often than not we won't get a clean bill of health. Jesus promised that after He went back to heaven, He would send the Holy Spirit, and the first thing the Spirit would do would be to convict us of sin (John 16:8). It goes without saying that being convicted of sin can and should put us on a guilt trip. This isn't particularly affirming, nor does it build self-esteem!

Some years ago, we got new furniture, one piece of which was a dressing table, sometimes called a vanity. I suppose this piece of furniture is called a vanity because it includes a mirror, and people consider those who spend time looking at themselves in a mirror to be vain. But looking into a mirror isn't all bad. We need some way to see ourselves. We wouldn't think of going out in public without first looking in the mirror—we might have spinach between our teeth!

Very few people get to see what we see in the mirror first thing every morning. It is no wonder that each year, people spend billions of dollars on products for eye care, teeth care, hair care, body care, and, of course, clothing. As a result, what people finally see of us is what we have managed to make of ourselves. (Some of us have more work to do than do others!)

An oft-quoted text says people look on the outward appearance, but God looks on the heart (1 Samuel 16:7). Personally, I don't mind people looking on my outward appearance. A person sometimes needs a reason to look their best, and I can make a big difference with a bar of soap, a shave, some deodorant, a haircut, and a suit of clothes. But what can we do when someone can see our heart, especially considering the kind of heart we have? Inasmuch as God looks on our heart, it would stand to reason that checking the condition of our heart regularly is even more critical than checking our personal appearance in a mirror.

Shouldn't we be as fastidious about what God sees in our families as we are with what others see in our physical appearance? Put another way, what would our family life be like if we were as conscientious about our attitudes toward our family members as we are toward our fellow employees or customers? The problems we have at home with our loved ones are potentially much more serious and have greater repercussions than having an occasional bad hair day.

When we get up in the morning, we go where we can face ourselves alone in the mirror. We know what it takes to look good and smell good. And when we have washed and groomed ourselves, we feel ready to meet the other members of the family and the rest of the world. Wouldn't it be even more helpful if, at the beginning of the day, we would do as Jesus did and go where we can be alone with God? We would, of course, want to bring along a mirror. When a person is alone with God, that mirror is the Bible.

In the story of Sleeping Beauty, the wicked queen looks into the mirror and asks, "Mirror, mirror on the wall, who's the fairest of them all?" When I look into the mirror of God's Word, the Holy Spirit doesn't tell me I am the fairest of them all. He convicts me of sin, of judgment, and of righteousness (John 16:8). Then He assures me that I am accepted in the Beloved (Ephesians 1:6). Sometimes I wish it were as easy to make our hearts smell clean and sweet as it is to bathe our bodies and dust on nice-smelling powder. But we can't change our heart, only God can do that in us and for us.

A new spouse

Sometimes when we look into a mirror, we see bitterness, resentment, depression, anger, or fear, and we think, *Oh, oh—I just saw a reflection of my wife* [or *my husband*].

Maybe we did. But if we're honest, most of the time we'll have to admit that we actually were seeing ourselves.

"But," someone objects, "you don't know my husband. The State of Florida has a lemon law. It says that when you buy a car that turns out to be a lemon, you can take it back. Pastor, I think I married a lemon. I need a new husband."

You may be absolutely correct. Maybe you do need a new husband. Maybe if I knew your husband as well as you do, I would agree with you. But there's always the possibility that he needs a new wife! As a minister of the gospel of the Lord Jesus Christ, I can guarantee that, as you begin to let Jesus make you what He wants you to be, you will soon find that you do have a new husband. I'm not exactly sure what he'll be like, but I know for sure that when your life begins to exhibit the character of Jesus, the other members of your family will change.

But a caution: We must allow God to bring changes into our own lives without condition. Often we are willing to make a conditional change. Our "contract"—which may be unspoken—goes something like this: "I'll change if he (or she) will change. But if he (or she) won't change, then I reserve the right to be what I've always been."

The fact is, I take a bath, I comb my hair, and I put on deodorant every day whether or not the other members of the family do. Sometimes all we can do is be the best we can be in our own life and hope that sooner or later the others will get the message. It could be later rather than sooner. I've heard of some family members who had to wait forty years for their loved ones to change. The Bible doesn't say "Here is the patience of the saints" for nothing! But it need not take that long for us to see a change in our own lives.

At the end of the day, salvation is a very personal thing. My salvation is not about my wife and me or the children and me or the grandchildren and me. My salvation is between Jesus and me. There is great comfort in the thought, "There hath no temptation taken you but such as is common to man: but God is faithful, who will not suffer you to be tempted above that ye are able; but will with the temptation also make a way to escape, that ye may be able to bear it" (1 Corinthians 10:13).

It's not my intention to determine where to place the blame for everything going on in our families. What I've been trying to say is that, before we do a study on what kind of people our spouses or our children ought to be, let's put first things first. Let's make a daily habit of looking at ourselves in the mirror of God's Word and asking ourselves what kind of people we ought to be. If God indeed needs to come in to change your home and mine, why shouldn't you and I be the first ones to open our hearts and let Him in? For starters, a changed home needs a changed me.

Points to Ponder
1. We are all born with a propensity to sin. Therefore, the environment in which we were raised didn't make us sinners but simply brought out the bad that was already in our nature.
2. Although the gospel is for everyone, we must see it as especially for us personally. In other words, no one needs grace more than I do.
3. Christ's crucifixion paid in full for the plan of salvation. But we will not be saved without our on-going cooperation.
4. Being well-groomed physically requires time and effort. Being well-groomed spiritually also requires time and effort.
5. The work of changing a family must begin somewhere. It might as well begin with me.

Homework Assignment
1. Make sure you have a personal quiet time with God each day.
2. We have toothpaste, powder, and deodorant to make us smell sweet. Choose three things you can do that will sweeten up the home environment for the other members of your family.

CHAPTER
5

Who's
the Boss?

*"Women hope men will change after marriage, but they don't;
men hope women won't change, but they do."*—Bettina Arndt

"Passionate sex is a symbol of a passionate relationship," says Barbara DeAngelis, author of *How to Make Love All the Time—The Secret for Making Love Work.*[1] Most men (and apparently Barbara DeAngelis) measure success in marriage by the yardstick of sex. But it's doubtful most wives do the same.

While sexual intimacy between husband and wife is meaningful as a symbol of the uniting of two lives into one, we should not see it as the foundation on which marriage is based. What should we consider the foundation of marriage? Most people would say love. That's part of the answer. But if marriage is based solely on love, what happens when one or the other spouse says "I don't love you anymore"?

The basis of the relationship of a man and a woman who choose to spend their lives together as husband and wife must be something other than their love for each other. Does this sound like heresy? Follow this line of thinking. Couples who live together without being married may indeed affirm their love for each other, but they're unwilling to make a commitment. It follows, then, that what sanctifies sexual intimacy is not just the love that the man and woman have for each other but also the lifelong commitment they've made. Commitment is the glue that holds a marriage together.

I'll never forget attending a village wedding in southern Asia, where my family and I lived for a number of years. Before the ceremony, we visited the young groom. He confessed that he wasn't acquainted with his bride but had managed to see her once from a distance. What happened in the little village church that afternoon was not so much about love but about commitment based on respect for their parents and for the institution of marriage. But in time, in that commitment, love was born.

I remember, too, a young man who was a member of the faculty at the mission school where I taught. He had fallen in love with a young woman and hoped his father would choose her to be his bride. But when the time came, the father chose someone else. The son was disappointed but resigned to accepting his father's judgment. After the wedding, the obedient son brought his new bride back to the campus. On the first Sabbath that they attended church together, the couple sat on the same pew but shyly, a little distance from each other—hardly what you would expect of newlyweds. Yet as the weeks and months went by, the pair began to sit closer together. The last I heard, their home was still a happy one. Commitment came first, but love was not far behind.

I can see you shaking your head and saying, "No way! I disagree. Besides, that is not our custom." This may be true, but romantic fantasies make a very poor glue for marriage.

These days, marriage is on a slippery slope. Whatever happened to the commitment to "love, honor and cherish 'til death do us part"? The United States Census Bureau's Statistical Abstract of the U.S. predicted in 2002 that 50 percent of all marriages would end in divorce. People are more likely to default on their marriage than on their mortgage. If marriage is to survive as the holy institution God ordained, it is imperative that we go to the Word of God and discover what He meant the relationship between husband and wife to be. To do less would be to institutionalize the status quo, to normalize the abnormal, and to accept the unacceptable.

In the beginning, marriage was between a man and a woman. "The Lord God said, It is not good that the man should be alone; I will make him an help meet for him. . . . Male and female created he them.

. . . And God blessed them, and God said unto them, Be fruitful, and multiply, and replenish the earth, and subdue it" (Genesis 2:18; 1:27, 28).

This relationship was unique. Unlike the mating of the majority of the other creatures in the animal kingdom, God meant the union between man and woman to be for life. Jesus reconfirmed the significance of the marriage commitment when He said, "For this cause shall a man leave father and mother, and shall cleave to his wife: and they twain shall be one flesh. Wherefore they are no more twain, but one flesh. What therefore God hath joined together, let not man put asunder" (Matthew 19:5, 6). God didn't create Adam and Eve and put them in the Garden to live together in the hope that their hormones would activate and they would fall in love. He created Eve and brought her to Adam in marriage—a relationship that was to last for life.

But God's original plan for marriage was short-circuited. An early perversion of this relationship was polygamy. Soon parents began to hear, "Get her for me; for she pleaseth me well" (Judges 14:3). And it wasn't long before women were relegated to second-class status and, at times, even treated as chattel—possessions.

Now, four thousand years later, the institution of marriage itself is at risk. Many have become increasingly tolerant of same-sex marriage, and, while not necessarily agreeing, are giving it tacit approval. People are setting aside the biblical norm for marriage and looking to society for cues regarding values and morals. The middle ground is fast disappearing. The time has come when people must decide which authority will mold their life—Scripture or the contemporary culture.

Equal—but not the same

The Constitution of the United States immortalized the concept that all persons "were created equal." But a quick look around reveals this cannot mean that all persons are the same. The Bible recognizes the differences between men and women, between husbands and wives. It also provides seamless principles by which these differences are to be recognized, respected, and protected.

In two significant passages, Scripture describes the relationship between husband and wife. One is 1 Peter 3:1-7:

> Likewise, ye wives, be in subjection to your own husbands; that, if any obey not the word, they also may without the word be won by the conversation of the wives; while they behold your chaste conversation coupled with fear. Whose adorning let it not be that outward adorning of plaiting the hair, and of wearing of gold, or of putting on of apparel; but let it be the hidden man of the heart, in that which is not corruptible, even the ornament of a meek and quiet spirit, which is in the sight of God of great price. For after this manner in the old time the holy women also, who trusted in God, adorned themselves, being in subjection unto their own husbands: even as Sara obeyed Abraham, calling him lord: whose daughters ye are, as long as ye do well, and are not afraid with any amazement.
>
> Likewise, ye husbands, dwell with them according to knowledge, giving honour unto the wife, as unto the weaker vessel, and as being heirs together of the grace of life; that your prayers be not hindered.

A liberated woman of the twenty-first century can easily get an "error message" in the computer of her mind when she reads this passage. It definitely doesn't fit the template of today's culture. But where shall we look for answers to our questions about marriage—to the Bible or to current culture? Many see the scriptural guidelines for marriage to be, at worst, discriminatory or, at best, outdated. Yet, in spite of society's purported wisdom concerning how to have a happy marriage, the family life of those following its norms is definitely deteriorating.

Without changing the original meaning of the passage I just quoted, a modern paraphrase might read:

> Husbands, remember that you and your wife are partners, sharing the grace of life. Be careful then how you treat

her. Though she may actually have more education than you do and have talents you don't have, God has ordained that she be the one who must bear the children. Because of this, she is vulnerable and must have your protection. Please don't take this assignment lightly, because failure to fulfill your responsibility to her will affect your relationship with God.

Wives, accept the protection of your husband even though your husband isn't fulfilling his role as spiritual leader in the home. While he may never read the Bible, there is the hope that one day he will become serious about spiritual things solely because of your influence in the home. The godly women of old, such as Abraham's wife, Sarah, respected their husbands. And don't let yourself get hung up on trying to be glamorous. God loves you as a person, and you don't want your husband to relate to you as a sex object. Impress him by the kind of woman you are.

Another passage rich with implications for the marriage relationship is Ephesians 5:22-27, 31-33:

Wives, submit yourselves unto your own husbands, as unto the Lord. For the husband is the head of the wife, even as Christ is the head of the church: and he is the saviour of the body. Therefore as the church is subject unto Christ, so let the wives be to their own husbands in everything.

Husbands, love your wives, even as Christ also loved the church, and gave himself for it; that he might sanctify and cleanse it with the washing of water by the word, that he might present it to himself a glorious church, not having spot, or wrinkle, or any such thing; but that it should be holy and without blemish.

For this cause shall a man leave his father and mother, and shall be joined unto his wife, and they two shall be one flesh. This is a great mystery: but I speak concerning Christ and the church. Nevertheless let every one of you in particular so love his wife even as himself; and the wife see that she reverence her husband.

There are men who are eager to use this text to prove that they have carte blanche as the head of the house. This would be an incorrect interpretation. In all His creation, God has established a chain of command. This chain begins in heaven, where there are orders of angels—the seraphim and the cherubim. The chain of command extends to this earth, where He made humankind the stewards of the rest of the creation.

In the marriage relationship that is based on a lifetime commitment between a man and a woman, the man is to be the protector of the family. The family, in turn, is called to submit itself to his protection. The husband, however, doesn't have intrinsic headship but derives his authority from Jesus, whose headship is founded on self-sacrificing love. A husband who tries to exercise authority after the manner of a dictator doesn't have a divine mandate. A husband who considers his wife to be his personal cook, laundry maid, babysitter, and sex partner and nothing more is making a big mistake.

God, who reads the heart, speaks to the weakness of husbands when, through the Holy Spirit, He commands them to love their wives. A husband's tendency is not to love his wife but to use her. When a man loves his wife, her purity should be his supreme concern. No one would ever want to defile a person he really loves. If we love our wives, we will hate anything that defiles her. Some men deliberately expose their wives to salacious films, magazines, or lewd and indecent images, thinking it's a justifiable way to put some spark into their romantic relationship. If a man draws his wife into anything that might tempt her, dishonor her, or debase her, he won't have the blessing of God.

While the Holy Spirit admonishes men to love their wives, it calls on wives to respect their husbands. Many wives claim they either will not or cannot respect their husbands. Yet the command is to respect them—not for who they are but for what they represent. Imagine, if you will, a highway patrol stopping my car. This particular officer's uniform is soiled and rumpled, and his attitude is disagreeable, so I tell him that I can ignore what he is saying because I don't like his looks or the way he speaks to me! Ridiculous. You see, it is not the person who must command my respect but what that person represents.

A drastic option

One day I was doing some carpentry work, and I hit my thumb with a hammer. Oh, how it hurt! At that moment I had a number of options. One option was to go to the emergency room and request that they cut off my arm at the shoulder. Less drastic, but still an option, would be to cut off my thumb.

"Who would be so foolish?" you may ask. But wait a moment. When a marriage seems headed toward the rocks, one could say divorce is an option—not always biblical, but an option nonetheless. Unfortunately, divorce now seems to be the option of choice. I have seen what divorce can do. Experience has borne out that the damage to the children (even adult children) can be permanent. They bear the scars forever. We need to remind ourselves that it was our Lord Himself who said, "What therefore God hath joined together, let not man [nor woman] put asunder" (Matthew 19:6).

Jesus predicted that in the last days the love of many would become cold (Matthew 24:12). We have interpreted this as having something to do with people leaving the church, and doubtless this is true. But the most telling fulfillment of this prophecy is what is happening to the love in our homes.

Although in the past, Western society might not have always followed Bible principles, it recognized them as the standard, and it bore their influence. Those days are largely past. The Bible is gathering dust on our shelves, and we are increasingly taking on secular and pagan values—and paying a price for doing so.

True love is not an involuntary feeling—a state into which people fall. It is an act of the will, based on commitment. Many who feel they have fallen out of love wrongly believe they can't do anything about it, so they give up on their marriage. But in these last days, God is calling husbands and wives to this deliberate, voluntary, committed love.

To love requires sacrifice, consideration, chivalry, communion, and courtesy—all resting on the foundation of commitment. Love is not dependent upon the lovability of its object. We didn't do anything that deserves Christ's love.

It appears we have two choices. Either we accept the Bible as the baseline guide for relationships between husbands and wives, or we follow the customs of our society. If we do the former, we will win. If we choose the latter, we will surely lose.

Points to Ponder
1. In marriage, love is nourished and protected by commitment.
2. Inasmuch as God determined that women would have the responsibility of bearing children, He commands men to protect them.
3. God calls men to a selfless headship of the family modeled after Christ's relationship to the church.
4. True love is not a feeling but a decision.
5. Marriage cannot endure if we accept the world's standards as our own.

Homework Assignment
1. If you are a husband, identify three ways you can demonstrate your love for your wife, other than physical intimacy.
2. If you are a wife, identify three ways you can demonstrate respect for your husband.

---

1. Barbara DeAngelis, *How to Make Love All the Time—The Secret for Making Love Work* (New York: Dell, 1987), 14.

CHAPTER

6

It's Your Call

"Never do for a child what he is capable of doing for himself."—Elizabeth G. Hainstock

Contrary to popular belief, the relationship that requires more quality time is not that of parent and child but of husband and wife. In trying to be the best parents in the world, many men and women have forgotten how to be good spouses. They've changed the focus of the home from being marriage-centered to being child-centered. This switch has brought negative results for both the marriage and the children. Many parents have become little more than servants to their children, hence the phenomenon of "soccer moms."

For the first eighteen months or so of a child's life, the parents treat her as if she were the only being on the face of the earth. The child yells, and they show up at her side, ready to serve. When she is uncomfortable, they make her comfortable. When she is hungry, they feed her. If she is having difficulty falling asleep, they rock her. By the time the child is eighteen months old, they've given her every reason to believe the world exists to fulfill her every desire.

Child-rearing "experts" advise parents to spend their time trying to make their children happy. Needless to say, many children have learned how to exploit this. While infants and toddlers obviously need a lot of attention, generally speaking, the more attention children get, the more they will demand.

Child-centered parents always act as if their first order of business is to "do" for their children. So, the challenge facing many families is not whether the parents shall pay attention to the child but whether the child shall pay attention to the parents.

Experience has shown that children won't pay adequate attention to parents who are paying too much attention to them. Many have found that the more they serve their children, the more the children will demand. Children whose parents overdose them with attention will clamor for even more. They can't get enough because they're getting too much in the first place.

Worldly wisdom suggests that the parents' foremost goal should be to make children feel good about themselves and to build their self-esteem. They're to accomplish this by paying a lot of attention to them and praising them while ignoring their inappropriate behavior. Parents are told they must protect their children from frustration and failure. The implication is that where there is a child with a problem, there is a mother, father, or teacher who is not giving the child enough attention and praise.

Consequently, the more parents pay attention to their children and the more they do for them, the more likely the children are to whine. On the other hand, when parents expect their children to do things for themselves and be responsible members of the family, the children are less likely to complain and can actually be a pleasure to have around.

Our parents of not so long ago provided us with what we *needed—* not necessarily with what we *wanted*. They may have said No more than they said Yes. They tried to raise us to stand on our own two feet. We were expected to come home from school, change our clothes, and find something to do. But times have changed. With the child-centered approach, we hear the lament, "Mom, I'm bored."

When I became old enough to work, my first job was to be a tender on a plastering crew. In those days, the tenders mixed the plaster and carried it in five-gallon buckets to the men who put it on the wall. We worked ten hours a day, six days a week. Mixing 80-pound bags of plaster and setting the buckets of plaster on the scaffold rendered membership at a health club unnecessary.

Sometimes the boss would show up on the job at three o'clock in the afternoon, when we'd been working since seven-thirty in the morning. "Let's get to work, boys," he would say.

We would answer, "John, we've been working all day. Where were you?"

His reply? "There is more to plastering than putting it on the wall." He was right, of course. Similarly, there's more to being a family than entertaining the children.

Respect for authority

While the foundation of the family was ordained to be divine love and commitment, what keeps the home functioning is respect for authority. Since the early 1960s, the concept of authority has been greatly eroded in our society. People now see themselves as the ultimate authority in just about everything. They think they must obey only themselves. This generation's loss of respect for authority has had a profound effect on the home.

People show their respect for authority through obedience, which is not natural but must be learned. The home is the place where children, who are born with a bent to selfishness and disobedience (Psalm 58:3), are to be taught the meaning of authority. Parents do this by teaching them to obey. Therefore, before children learn anything else, they should be taught obedience. Of course, parents must do this in the context of a warm, loving relationship.

A mother, for instance, can't teach obedience by saying things like "Honey, don't you think you ought to clean your room now?" She's likely to hear something like "Wait until this TV program is over." This easily results in the mother yelling at the child—or maybe even giving up and deciding it would be easier to clean the room herself.

Some of the methods used these days for raising children do not teach obedience but rather suggest negotiation. The way we communicate with our children often invites debate. Instead of being the ones in charge, we increasingly find ourselves trying to get the children to "sign-off" on what we want them to do.

Sometimes the boss on my old plastering crew would say, "Dick, would you mind doing such and such?" Many times when I was tired or busy doing something else, I wanted to say, "Yes, I do mind." Of course, he never expected a reply to his question. I recognize now he was being polite. But giving a command by asking a question about how a person feels about the matter doesn't necessarily teach obedience. On the other hand, when my boss said to me, "Dick, move the scaffold to the next room," I would simply respond, "OK," and do it. As the older and wiser men on the job would say, "Yours is not to reason why, yours it is to do or die." That may sound heartless and out of step with current thought; nevertheless, parents can become so sensitive to the feelings of their children that they find it difficult to teach obedience.

Children can expect explanations, but they often demand more. As a rule, children ask the reason behind an adult's decision when they don't like the decision. They almost never ask for a reason when an adult decision is to their liking.

If we are to prepare our children for successful lives both here and in the life to come, we must teach them not only to obey but also to understand that disobedience brings consequences—a basic element of the great controversy between good and evil. So, to be effective in teaching our children to obey, we must teach them

- where we came from (God created us),
- why we are the way we are (Sin marred God's perfect plan.),
- what we can do to change, and
- what our destiny is.

Obedience is essential not only for the distant by-and-by but also for holding a job in the here-and-now. And it goes without saying that if children don't learn to respect human authority, they won't respect God's authority.

Although by nature no one likes being told what to do, it is a sign of maturity when one accepts being told what to do by legitimate authority. The earlier children learn this, the less grief they will suffer. The first authority children encounter is that of their parents. If the children don't learn to accept their parents' authority, they'll find it all but impossible to accept any authority whatsoever.

Every child's main responsibility is to obey his or her parents. A child's dislike of some decision an adult has made is no indication that the decision or action in question was wrong. In a sense, it might be said that parents are not to please the child; rather, the child is to learn to please the parents. When the Bible discusses the role of children in the family, the emphasis is on responsibilities, not rights. Two texts that illustrate this point are Ephesians 6:1, "Children, obey your parents in the Lord: for this is right," and Colossians 3:20, "Children, obey your parents in all things: for this is well pleasing unto the Lord."

Thousands of books have been written on how parents should discipline their children. While many people consider discipline to mean punishment, it has a much broader meaning. To *discipline* means to make someone a *disciple*—in other words, to teach. Discipline, then, is the process of raising our children. It is the process by which parents make disciples of their children. A disciple is someone who will follow the lead of a teacher, a legitimate authority. How can we expect our children to follow our lead if we haven't first convinced them that they are to pay attention to us rather than the other way around?

Parents can accomplish this goal through establishing reasonable yet challenging expectations, setting and enforcing limits, and perhaps most important of all, modeling appropriate behavior. It goes without saying that self-disciplined adults will be the most successful at disciplining their children.

Effective punishment

While discipline is not necessarily punishment, punishing inappropriate behavior is an unavoidable part of the overall process. When our children do something wrong, we must make sure our response isn't destructive. Our response should reflect the seriousness of the misdeed, but we should avoid calling names. It's better to say "I am disappointed in what you've done" than to say "You're such a dumbbell." It's better to say "I'm scared to think about your having acted that way" than to say "You're never going to learn."

We should also avoid overreacting in other ways too. We must not allow our feelings to go out of control. God has feelings about sinners, but He doesn't lose control. We may need to wait to react to the misdeed until we have enough perspective to see it in proper perspective. In times of relational crisis, taking our time can actually be in our favor.

Another challenge a parent faces is the tendency to overreact. Too often we put up with our children's misbehavior until we reach the breaking point, and then we become unglued. Think very carefully before you make plans to "get tough." You use the best kind of toughness when you let your children experience real and appropriate consequences of their actions. Children must learn the principle of cause and effect. Reactions on your part that grow out of anger and the desire to punish are likely to be inappropriate. Punishment motivated by anger only generates anger and a desire to strike back in the child's heart. Therefore,

- don't impose a consequence while in the heat of anger,
- make sure you choose a consequence you can enforce,
- try to make the consequence fit the crime, and
- make sure you know how the child will perceive the consequence.

While doing these things, we should continue to be aware that the goal of corrective discipline is not to break the child's will but to bend it and to direct it.

What about spanking as a method of discipline? In her article, "When to Spank," Lynn Rosellini provided an interesting perspective. She wrote,

> One lesson of the spanking controversy is that whether parents spank or not matters less than how they spank. A single disapproving word can bring a sensitive child to tears, while a more spirited youngster might need stronger measures. . . . Spankings should be done in private to spare children humiliation and without anger. [1]

Society increasingly frowns on using corporeal punishment on children, and not without cause. Physical abuse of children is not tolerated and is severely punished by the courts.

The Bible weighs in on the issue of spanking:

> He that spareth his rod hateth his son: but he that loveth him chasteneth him betimes (Proverbs 13:24).
>
> The rod and reproof give wisdom: but a child left to himself bringeth his mother to shame (Proverbs 29:15).
>
> Foolishness is bound in the heart of a child; but the rod of correction shall drive it far from him (Proverbs 22:15).

I remember well one spanking I received, though there must have been many others. This particular time I was six years old. It was Sabbath, and I was dressed in short pants. After the worship service, I sat on the ground in front of the church and began rubbing dirt on my legs. My parents told me to stop. Apparently I didn't stop, because the next thing I knew my dad advised me that after sunset I was going to get a spanking with a switch. That day I wished I could be like Joshua when he prayed that the sun would stand still!

I spent the afternoon trying to find a switch for my dad to use. Of course, I brought some old, dry sticks that were sure to break very easily. Alas, the sun didn't stand still, and the moment of truth finally arrived. Dad found his own willow switch, and it did what it was supposed to do.

The foremost obligation of parents is to give children all they truly need, along with a small amount of what they want. Fifty years ago a child may have had five toys. Today, by the age of five, a child may have hundreds. Many of the modern toys do not encourage children to be creative. While children of today are often heard saying how bored they are, children of yesterday would play for hours with pots and pans or in an empty cardboard box. Some of us remember those days. Even now, when I am trimming two-by-fours, my wife will collect the leftover pieces of wood blocks for the grandchildren to play with when they come to visit. And not surprisingly, when they do come over, they head for the blocks first.

In the final analysis, the goal of making disciples of our children is not to make them subservient and dependent but autonomous and self-reliant. They should be guided in learning how to solve problems on their own, how to tolerate frustration, how to persevere in face of adversity, and, in general terms, how to stand on their own two feet. For more than twenty years, a part of my ministry had to do with Community Services. Through the years, I learned we ought not to help the needy as much as we can but only to the point where they can help themselves. The same principle applies in the family.

Recently I updated my home office, which meant I bought new office furniture. I overlooked one small detail—the new furniture was delivered unassembled. Putting it all together was not something I could do with my eyes closed. The directions were clear, but I had to follow them closely. When I did, I was pleased with the finished product.

I wish raising children were that easy. My office furniture came precut and predrilled. Unfortunately, children don't come that way. True, as parents, we say our work is cut out for us. Yet the parts do not always fit, and little ones are not inclined to sit still during the years when we are trying to put them together. In some ways, raising children is like trying to change a flat tire without pulling the car off the road.

While parenting, we will face hereditary and environmental forces beyond our control. One thing is clear: We must partner with God and with His Word. By His grace, we should make it our goal to raise obedient and God-fearing children and to guide them into self-reliance.

Points to Ponder

1. The greatest gifts you can give your children are the legacy of your faith in God and the security of a home in which the parents have a stable marriage.
2. Obedience and respect for authority are requisites for success.
3. There is a lot of wisdom in the old adage, "Children are to be seen and not heard."
4. Explain your requirements, but don't let your children argue with you about them. Parents are responsible for their children, but children are accountable to their parents.

5. We should not discipline our children when we are angry.

Homework Assignment

1. Decide two qualities that you wish for your children. Then, for the next month, intentionally model these behaviors in your own life.
2. Determine that for the next month you will not discipline when you are angry. In other words, don't strike while the hammer is hot!

Note: I've given these assignments in the time frame of one month because it usually takes a month to form a new habit.

Recommended Reading

I've found the book *A Family of Value,* by John Rosemond, to be insightful and helpful.

---

1. Lynn Rosellini, "When to Spank," *U.S. News and World Report,* April 13, 1998.

CHAPTER
7

You're a Big Girl Now

"Do unto others as you would have them do unto you."—Jesus

If you thought the terrible two's were difficult, wait until you've been through the five thousand days it takes for children to pass through the pre-teens, teens, and young adulthood! As an older parent, I've been there and done that. Occasionally when I'm in a supermarket or other public venue and see a mother with little children in tow, I'll approach her and say, "Enjoy these baby years!"

National Public Radio's *Morning Edition* of May 30, 2002, featured a program entitled, "Amish Teens Tested in the 'Devil's Playground!' " The program revealed that when Amish teenagers turn sixteen, their parents set them free to explore the good and bad of their contemporary society. They're allowed a taste of the outside world. The Amish call this time *rumspringa*, which, in Pennsylvania German, means "running around." The period can last from a few months to a few years. One day they are under their parents' command; the next, they can do whatever they want. They're left to decide for themselves whether to stay modern or to return to the old-fashioned ways—often a decision over which they struggle. Interestingly, approximately 85 to 90 percent of them eventually choose to join the church.

Although American culture doesn't have a formal rite of passage, children make a transition nonetheless. Parents and grandparents may not make it happen, but they can't keep it from happening either. We can't control the decisions our young people make (we make a mistake if we try to do that), but we can support them and give them gentle steering currents. Sometimes I wonder which is the most stressful: being a teen or being the parent of one. While a teen has to cope with huge physical, emotional, and social changes, parents must transition from being in total control of their children's lives to what may appear to be a total loss of control.

Years ago, my wife and I raised dogs as a hobby. We raised both poodles and Dobermans. From time to time, we would have to administer a pill to one of the animals. That's quite a process. First, one must manually open the animal's mouth. Then, while holding the pill between the index finger and the thumb, one must somehow get past the sharp, gnashing teeth and lay the pill as far back on the tongue as possible. Then one must quickly close the animal's mouth and begin massaging the throat. With a little luck, the dog will swallow, and down the hatch goes the pill. (I won't even try to imagine what it's like to give a pill to a cat!)

Sometimes I think it is as delicate and challenging a job to get a teen to do the right thing as it is to get a dog to swallow a pill. It takes practice and infinite patience. While parents cannot always control their teens, they must always control themselves. The teen's behavior may not be predictable, but the adult's behavior should be.

This chapter will not so much explore how to solve problems with teens (which may not be possible) as it will suggest how to get a handle on some of the problems adults have in relating to teenagers and young adults (which is possible).

One hundred teens

My wife and I no longer have teenagers in our home, but we do have teens in our lives. They're our grandchildren. Therefore, my perspective on this matter is not limited to retrospect and past experience; it comes from the current need to know how to relate as a grandparent. In addition, because I wanted to understand better teen thinking, I prepared a questionnaire that I handed out to one hundred twelfth-grade students at a Christian high school. Ninety-nine of the hundred students completed the questionnaire.

My questionnaire contained only three questions. First, I asked the teens to rate their relationship with their parents on a scale of one to ten. I was encouraged to see that barely a handful scored below a five. Most rated their relationship between seven and ten. This is significant because it indicates that the answers to the subsequent questions were based on sincerity and good will, not bitterness and resentment.

Question 2 was: "What do you feel parents could do to improve the relationship with their teens?" I provided spaces for three suggestions per student. Question 3 was: "What do you wish your parents understood about teens?" Again, I provided room for three responses. I didn't intend the survey to be scientifically valid. Instead, I meant it to capture the feelings and convictions of a large group of teens.

I've distilled the responses to question 2 into two groups: do's and don'ts.

Do:
- ask questions in a calm way
- encourage us
- try to listen, and act as if you understand
- take more time to understand our feelings
- give us more freedom and space
- explain, don't just give commands
- laugh more
- be friendlier and more respectful
- show love
- make sure you get the whole story from everyone
- show trust
- hold fast to your guidelines, but be reasonable
- be more open-minded
- let us take more responsibility
- talk to us, be our friend, and be genuine
- pray with us
- be a little more lenient and trusting
- be nice and kind

- give advice because you're experienced, not just to show authority
- be an example; don't be hypocritical
- allow us to grow up
- think of teens as what we are—not kids and not adults
- be more compassionate
- listen more and talk less
- get involved in our activities

Don't:
- criticize us so much
- nag us at every little thing
- make us feel stupid when we mess up
- compare us to yourself when you were growing up
- put us down
- be so quick to yell at us
- be quick to punish
- assume things so quickly
- compare us to other kids
- work so much
- be so strict
- say harsh words
- jump to conclusions
- hold something over our heads (Instead, help us to learn from our mistakes.)
- be overbearing

As I summarized this list of do's and don'ts, it was apparent that the points the teens expressed were not only right but reasonable and could generally be substantiated from the Sermon on the Mount, 1 Corinthians 13, the book of Proverbs, and several chapters from Ephesians!

Things teens wish their parents understood:
- Communication is everything.
- We're sensitive.
- We're not totally unpredictable.

- We're all messy.
- We experience stress.
- We're just going through a phase.
- We want to serve others.
- Things are different from when they were young.
- They don't need to keep reminding us of things.
- We do care about them and value their opinions; we just wish they wouldn't offer them so often.
- We're not all involved in bad things; we wish they would start thinking positive!
- Privacy is very important to us.
- We're embarrassed when they show naked baby pictures to everyone.
- We want love, and that even though we don't say it, we want them to be there for us.
- We wish they weren't so suspicious.
- We want to hang out with our friends by ourselves sometimes— and that's not because we hate our younger brothers or sisters.
- We're not our siblings; don't expect us to act like them.
- We're going to grow up eventually, and it's not a sin to try new things.
- We don't always express how much we care; we do care, even when we don't say so.
- We have mood swings, and they may not understand why.
- We're still learning about life.
- We make mistakes.
- Life is short; so we don't want to argue.
- We'll rebel if they're too strict.
- The more they hassle us, the less likely we are to do what they want us to.
- We don't need them to check on us continually.
- We're not little kids anymore.
- We're not all stupid.
- Sometimes we have to learn the hard way—as they did.
- Just because we don't tell them every detail of our lives doesn't mean that we're hiding something.

- They turn us off when they repeat themselves as if we're little children and they don't trust us.
- We're human too, and we wish they'd be proud of us.
- We're not perfect, but we're trying to do the best we can.
- We're dealing with things they didn't have to when they were our age.
- We have feelings.
- They shouldn't blame teens for everything bad that happens; sometimes bad things just happen.
- Sometimes we yell for attention; teens have bad days too.
- We want approval; we want to feel good about ourselves; and we want to make them proud.

The feelings expressed in the responses to my short questionnaire speak to principles that apply not only to the parent/teen relationship but also to the relationship between spouses or friends in general. If adults would work to implement the principles expressed by these young people, the result would be stronger, happier families. The truth is that parents don't need a university degree in adolescent psychology or interpersonal relations to raise children. The principles of the gospel, consistently applied in the home, will be sufficient.

Be kinder

"If I had my life to live all over again," a friend once confided, "I think I would be more kind." I've never forgotten those words. It's time we stopped judging, worrying, punishing, and becoming angry with our young people. That behavior isn't working anyway. I'm convinced that things would be completely different in the home if we were consistently kind.

Probably the most family-changing text in Scripture is Ephesians 4: 31, 32: "Let all bitterness, and wrath, and anger, and clamour, and evil speaking, be put away from you, with all malice: And be ye kind one to another, tenderhearted, forgiving one another, even as God for Christ's sake hath forgiven you."

Friendship must be based on mutual respect and esteem. What would our relationship with our teens be like if we treated them with the same kindness and deference that we show our friends? Or put another way, what would our homes be like if we were as kind to those we love as we are to total strangers?

Sometimes parents try to control teens by putting them on a guilt trip. But guilt is a poor motivator and can have damaging and lasting effects. Trying to govern teens by threatening them is equally ineffective. It usually results in making them more secretive. And trying to control teens by comparing them to other teens or with their siblings will result in resentment and feelings of inadequacy.

While rules and regulations are necessary, our relationship with our teens must be based on love and good will. The better our relationship with them, the better we feel as parents. The better their relationship with us, the better they'll feel about themselves. Building such a relationship is not a science. No two people will take exactly the same path. The important thing is the direction. Whatever brings closeness, caring, and communication will get you closer to where you want to go.

Even normal teenagers have lower lows and higher highs than adults do, and they probably have no idea where these feelings come from. Experience has shown that nagging teenagers about their moods makes things worse. In general, it's better to treat your moody teen like a beloved houseguest who is going through a tough time and who needs a great deal of privacy!

Many parents feel it is wrong to praise young people for doing what they ought to do in the first place. But you will find it is better to move away from an emphasis on reacting to bad behavior and, instead, to search for and praise good behavior. That's a sure way of improving the atmosphere in your home.

Proverbs 18:24 contains a profound truth: "A man that hath friends must shew himself friendly." Your best friend doesn't have influence over you because he (or she) demands it or is the smartest person in the world. Your friend has influence over you because the two of you talk to each other, and you trust your friend because he (or she) has let you know that he (or she) cares about you. Take this to heart if you want to be able to influence your teen.

Could it be that we often fail in our relationships with those we love because we maintain a double standard? Someone once said that he couldn't wait until he got home at night because he was tired of being kind all day. It seems easier or more important to keep things together everywhere else but at home. We have people skills with everyone but the members of our immediate family. The burden of this book is to proclaim that the time has come, yea is overdue, when we must allow the Holy Spirit to implement the principles of grace in our homes. As we do this, the hearts of the fathers and mothers will be turned to the teens, and the hearts of the teens to their parents. Not only this, there will be a wonderful transformation in relationship between husband and wife and between brother and sister.

When our kids are grown and gone, we're likely to say, "I wish we'd been closer. I wish we hadn't fought so much. I wish we had communicated more. I wish I'd gotten to know my kids better. I wish I'd shown more care instead of always criticizing them." Now, when they're home, is the time to do what you can to avoid having those regrets.

Points to Ponder
1. During the teen years, our children are preparing themselves to leave home and are discovering who they will be as independent persons.
2. Our influence over our teens is only as strong as our ability to communicate effectively with them.
3. We'll know our teens trust us when they feel safe sharing bad news.
4. Just because a teen appears not to care doesn't mean they don't.
5. Generally, we should treat teens as if they're friends who happen to be going through a difficult time of their life.

Homework Assignment
1. Express appreciation to your teens at least three times a week, and tell them every day you love them. (If you don't have a teen in your home, do these things for your spouse!)

2. When you lose your cool, make sure you ask your teens for for-giveness.

Recommended Reading

Parent/Teen Breakthrough, by Mira Kirshenbaum and Charles Foster, is a helpful book on how to develop a healthy relationship with your teen.

CHAPTER
8

Till Death Do Us Part

"Cast me not off in the time of old age; forsake me not when my strength faileth."–King David

When my wife and I married, one of us was nineteen and the other was twenty. I'm not going to tell you which of us is older, because when I do, she becomes angry! Anyway, my pastor dad officiated at our wedding. During the rehearsal he told me that when I kissed the bride, I was to make it short and sweet. Apparently, when he was attending a wedding as a young man, the bridal couple kissed so long and passionately that the guests almost felt they should close their eyes. I told my dad not to worry, but he was taking no chances. We have an audiotape of the service, and it reveals that when Dad pronounced us "man and wife" and I kissed the bride, he muttered, "That's enough!"

So there we stood in June 1960, as bright as newly minted pennies as Dad asked us if we would be faithful until death should us part. When you're young and no one close to you has died, this part of the vow doesn't seem to have a lot of relevance. The only old person I remembered in my immediate family was Grandma. In fact, I can't remember when she wasn't old. In the eyes of a child, Grandma is always old. Children figure Grandma must have been born old!

There was a time in our culture when old age was revered—or, if not revered, at least respected. In those days, we wouldn't think of addressing our elders by their first names. It was always Grandma Nelson and Uncle Henry. Times have changed. Old is out, young is in. Everything seems to orbit around being young and staying young. Some seem to have concluded that they will always be young. When I preach, I often have to remind the younger generation that I wasn't born with white hair. The truth is that, like it or not, even the younger generation are themselves Old Age Positive. They may not have any symptoms now, but they'll begin to manifest them when they get to be about forty-five years of age.

When I went to my twenty-fifth class reunion at Mount Vernon Academy, I discovered that the majority of us were actually better looking at forty-two than we were at seventeen. But just three or four years later, things began to change. I'm refusing to go to any more class reunions because my classmates' eyesight has gotten so bad that they hardly recognize me!

My father-in-law was a handsome man. In his later years, he confessed that sometimes when he looked at himself in the mirror, he would think, "What happened to me?" Next time you visit someone in a convalescent home, notice the photographs on the chest of drawers. No, they weren't born old.

I don't know who came up with the bit about old age being the golden years. As far as I can figure, it must have been someone who made a million dollars selling cemetery lots. They say old age is all in your mind. I wish someone would tell that to my face and my back. I was looking at my birth certificate the other day, and I discovered that it has an expiration date! The same is true for you. We made it alive out of the twentieth-century, but we won't survive the twenty-first.

Perhaps you've reached the time of life when your spouse is gone, your kids have moved away or don't visit, and you pray every night that the Lord will let you go to your rest. No wonder the Bible refers to this time not as the golden years but as the "evil days." I used to think that Ecclesiastes 12 was a chapter about young people because it begins, "Remember now thy creator in the days of thy youth." Back when we were in school, that's all we had to memorize. However, the rest of the chapter is not about youth at all but is a poetic description of old age. The Clear Word paraphrase decodes the symbolism of verses 1-8 this way:

Remember your Creator while you're still young and give Him the best of your life. The years pass quickly, and soon you'll be old and will say to yourself, "I surely don't enjoy life like I used to." When those days come, your eyesight will grow dim, and you will see little difference between a bright sunny day and a moonlit night. The stars will fade from your view, and each day the sky will seem overcast and dark, filled with clouds of rain. Your arms that were so strong and quick to protect you will shake and tremble. Your legs will grow weak. Your teeth will fall out, and it will be hard for you to chew. Your eyes will be looking through half-drawn shutters. Your ears will not pick up the noise on the streets, and you will barely hear the mill as it grinds out the wheat or the singing of birds in the morning. The music of young girls will be stilled.

You'll be afraid of heights and of falling in the street. Your hair will turn as white as the blossoms of an almond tree, and you'll drag yourself along and rest after each step like an old grasshopper rests after each hop. Your desire for everything in life will fail. You'll be heading for your last resting place. People will mourn for you just as they mourned for others before you, and there will be no turning back.

The silver chain that holds you to your loved ones will finally break, and the golden lamp of life will go out. The rope on the pulley of life's well will finally snap, and the pitcher full of the water of life will fall and break. Your body will decay and return to dust, and the spark of life which God gave you will go back to Him. Life is futile because what you do doesn't last. Let me say it again, life is futile because what you do doesn't last.

The picture painted in these verses make it difficult to conclude that old age is all in the mind!

Old age and the family

What does the subject of old age have to do with the family? Everything, because we're all headed toward old age. A person who doesn't take into account the reality of life described in Ecclesiastes 12 is in denial. Life is a continuum. Someone put it this way, "We are born, we struggle, and then we die." That may sound a little harsh, but it's not far from the truth. I myself have reached the time when I see life from the summit of a mountain, as it were. From this vantage point, I can see down both sides. I can see where I've been, and I can see where I'm headed.

Part of descending the other side of the mountain is experiencing the passing of our parents. Both my parents are gone now. A few years ago my father-in-law died of an aneurism. My mother-in-law died from a stroke at the ripe old age of 92, but not before suffering the heartache of dementia.

Regarding dementia, a hospital chaplain once gave me a bit of sage advice. Having passed through something similar with her mother, she suggested that when old folks act childish, be a child with them. I believe she was right. After all, that is the way we interact with children. But acting childish with a child is one thing; doing so with your mother is something else.

It is difficult to know how to relate to our parents when they come to the end of their lives. It saddens me to hear how often grown children don't visit their parents who are in convalescent homes. Many times this isn't because they don't care; it's because they can't bear to watch the changes that old age brings. Since they can't cope with it, they avoid going where they see it.

Life is a mix of both the good and bad. Though sometimes when our children were little, we thought they would drive us crazy, I think those were really the easiest years. We were young and strong, and our parents were well and prospering. Now my children are grown and gone and have challenges of their own. My wife and I have shared with them the pain of divorce; we have embraced a grandchild with a pierced eyebrow; and we have mourned a mother who at times couldn't remember the names of our children.

I've noticed that getting older doesn't necessarily mean becoming nicer and kinder, though we might hope that would be the case. As the years pass, inhibitions that might have helped keep people on track tend to fall away, and they can easily fall into the habit of being bruisingly brunt. Old age tends not to be a time of flexibility but of becoming set in one's ways. After years of hard work, disappointment, and even bitterness, spouses can find themselves taking out their frustrations on each other. Some senior couples talk to each other in shocking ways. I'm praying that in my final years, I'll be kind to my wife. You might also want to start practicing for those years now.

My father's generation sincerely believed that Jesus was coming in their day. They believed He would deliver them before they died, and they organized their lives around the Blessed Hope. They were sure they were among those who would be "alive and remain." But alas, the majority of them have now gone to their rest to await the resurrection. The apparent delay in the return of our Lord has resulted in an even greater disappointment than the Great Disappointment of 1844. It's greater simply because more people are awaiting His coming now than were then. Like our parents, we'll have to face the fact that we might have to pass to our rest.

We used to play a game called "The Prince of Paris Has Lost His Hat." Someone would begin by saying, "The prince of Paris lost his hat, and number three has it." If you were number three, the idea was to say quickly without getting tongue-tied, "Who, sir? Me, sir? No, sir; not I, sir. Number 6 has it." Then it was Number 6's turn to answer. We live in a culture that is playing a blame game. The in thing is to blame our parents, be they living or dead, for whatever problems we may have. What we forget is that, even if our parents were less than perfect, the fifth commandment requires us to respect them.

When I remember my parents, I thank God for all the good they were to me. Then, often, I ask God to forgive them for mistakes they may have made. Of course, I don't believe in praying for the dead, but I pray this way because I want my heart to be merciful and forgiving about mistakes that I might otherwise be inclined to blame on them. There will be few, if any, changes for the better in our lives until we're willing to own up to our problems. No more of the blame game.

Though we spend our lives trying to avoid death, there comes a time when it is a welcome relief from the pain and vicissitudes of life. So it was with my parents. At the time, death seemed a welcome relief.

But in reality, it is an enemy that leaves a loneliness that continues until the trumpet sounds and the dead in Christ rise.

I apologize if this chapter seems to be excessively depressing. By now, you must realize that I am speaking mostly to the difficult situations. Why? Because those are the ones most often brought to my attention. In my own life, I am currently in the midst of a reality check. If I read Ecclesiastes 12:1 correctly, the sooner we get an accurate picture of life, the better we will live. I believe that the greatest and surest crisis of the human sojourn is old age, and the first part of life is about getting ready for the inevitable. I'm not saying that I don't believe in the soon coming of Jesus. But until His return, the fact remains that, with only a few exceptions, the mortality rate for the human race is 100 percent.

Pure, undefiled religion

Earlier, I explained that I included this chapter about old age because old people are still family members. But there is another important aspect that goes beyond the immediate family to the church family. For a number of years I supervised the Community Services department in the conference where I worked. I used to challenge the volunteers with the text, "Pure religion and undefiled before God and the Father is this, to visit the fatherless and widows in their affliction, and to keep himself unspotted from the world" (James 1:27).

It is sobering to realize that a pure, undefiled religion has to do with the way we relate to widows, who seem to comprise most of the aged among us. Whatever else you may decide to do to minister to the suffering and needy, please don't forget the shut-ins, especially those in convalescent homes. Notice, the text in James doesn't tell us to give money to the widows, though that might be the need from time to time. It tells us to visit them. While generosity with our money shows that we care, generosity with our time requires even greater care. If there is one group above all others deserving of the gift of our time, it is the aged.

Yes, as I stood beside my beautiful bride, the words "'til death do you part" seemed to reach far into the future. But those words are very meaningful to me now. From where I stand, I realize that, in a unique way, the old people in the family are just as important as the young. I haven't forgotten the joy and even the pain of raising children. But now I know something of the joy and, yes, even the pain of old age in the family. I look forward to seeing my parents again when all things are made new.

"I John saw the holy city, the New Jerusalem, coming down from God out of heaven, prepared as a bride adorned for her husband. And I heard a great voice out of heaven saying, Behold, the tabernacle of God is with men, and he will dwell with them, and they shall be his people, and God himself shall be with them, and be their God.

"And God shall wipe away all tears from their eyes; and there shall be no more death, neither sorrow, nor crying, neither shall there be any more pain: for the former things are passed away" (Revelation 21:2-4).

Even so, come Lord Jesus.

Points to Ponder
1. The mortality rate for our race is 100 percent.
2. Old age is doubtless the greatest burden we will carry in our sojourn on this earth.
3. God commands us to honor our parents regardless of what kind of parents they were for the simple reason that He used them to create us.
4. Old age doesn't necessarily strengthen character; it reveals it.
5. Churches should give high priority to their ministry to their senior citizens—it's important.

Homework Assignment
1. Ask your pastor who in the church could provide you a list of shut-in members.
2. Find others who will help you visit the shut-ins regularly, particularly on Sabbath.

Recommended Reading
Caring for the Aged, from Focus on the Family, is an important resource book for those caring for elderly family members.

CHAPTER
9

Single,
but Not Alone

*"A father of the fatherless, and a judge [defender] of the widows,
is God in his holy habitation."*—King David

As you know, Malachi 4:5, 6 provided the inspiration for this book. These verses say, "Behold, I will send you Elijah the prophet before the coming of the great and dreadful day of the Lord: and he shall turn the heart of the fathers to the children, and the heart of the children to their fathers, lest I come and smite the earth with a curse." There is one small glitch in this description of family reconciliation: More than 9.8 million children in the United States live with a mother but no father, and another 2.1 million live with a father and no mother.[1]

We must acknowledge the fact that the single-parent home is fast becoming a regular feature of society. Consequently, the single-parent family has become an important component of church life. Many people have a difficult time admitting this fact because it does not reflect God's ideal plan for the home. Yet, as time goes on, we can expect to see the number of singles in the church increasing. This group includes those who are divorced as well as those who are single because of the death of a spouse. And, of course, some are single because they have never married. In fact, we all begin life as singles, and at least half of us will be single again during the final years of our life.

I don't pretend to be an expert on the subject of being a single parent or of singleness in general. Though I haven't personally experienced divorce nor am I a child of divorce, I do know something of the grief that results, having experienced it up close.

I hope you will forgive my frankness on this very difficult subject. But a book on the family in these last days would be remiss not to include a chapter acknowledging the growing phenomena of the single parent. Though family situations may differ, the God-given principles apply to everyone, married or single. God is no respecter of persons, and neither must we be.

The first single mother recorded in Scripture was Hagar. Abraham's relationship with his wife's servant is not a model for what people should do if they can't produce children. After Sarah had her own son, the already bad situation came to a head, and Abraham, the biological father, sent Ishmael and his mother away into the desert with only a little food and water, which were soon gone. The young boy was at the point of death, and his mother, who couldn't bear to watch him die, was weeping when God intervened. Not only did God save their lives, but the record also says God was with the boy as he grew up (Genesis 21:20).

The Bible mentions other single parents. There was, for example, the widow who appealed to the prophet Elisha because the people to whom she owed money wanted to sell her sons as slaves to pay the debt (2 Kings 4). And one of the most touching stories in all Scripture tells of a man engaged to a girl whom he discovers is pregnant. In those days, engagement had the same legal force as marriage. We can only imagine what must have gone on in Joseph's mind as he struggled with whether or not he should "divorce" Mary. So, Jesus' home situation was that of a blended family. Later, Mary may have become a single parent. Scripture refers several times to her and to Jesus' brothers but not to Joseph, implying that he was dead, and we don't know how early in Jesus' life he died.

One of the first issues facing the early Christian church involved singles. Church leaders struggled with the question of how to minister effectively to them. They met the challenge by appointing seven deacons and giving guidelines as to who would qualify to receive help.

The matter of divorce

Nowadays, divorce is responsible for many of the single-parent families in our society. When divorce was less common in the church, members who weren't divorced often kept their distance from those who were. Now, those who have experienced divorce may include our parents, our sons or daughters, our brothers, sisters, grandchildren— or even us. Divorce is no respecter of families, religious affiliations, income levels, or educational backgrounds.

People who have gone through this experience say that to them it was worse than the death of a loved one—worse in the sense that death is out of our control, while divorce is a type of death by choice. In other words, it is a rejection.

One of the most immediate and potentially long-lasting results of divorce is bitterness and anger, which, if not dealt with, will effect a chain reaction. Former spouses often spend the first months or even years after their divorce screaming at each other. They may feel justified in venting, but their children are the losers; even though the former spouses are no longer husband and wife, they will always be Mom and Dad. The sooner they adjust—however painfully—to their new relationship, the better it will be for all concerned.

Even grandparents can be unwittingly pulled into the trap of bitterness and recrimination. Yet that need not happen. I have a former son-in-law who still calls me Dad, and he is right. Though he's no longer the husband of my daughter, he will always be the father of my grandchildren. I can testify how important it is to continue to pray for former sons- and daughters-in-law. How can God save our grandchildren if we see their mother or father as the enemy?

Many things happen to us over which we have no control. Often, divorce is one of them. While we can't always control whether or not it happens to us, we do have the choice as to how we'll react to it— whether we'll become angry, bitter, and resentful or whether we'll follow our Savior, "who, when he was reviled, reviled not again; when he suffered, he threatened not; but committed himself to him that judgeth righteously" (1 Peter 2:23).

The prevalence of divorce highlights how careful people should be in choosing whom they will marry. When people buy a home, they follow a lengthy process that includes an inspection of both the property and the title. However, rarely are they as careful when choosing the person with whom they expect to spend the rest of their life.

Benjamin Franklin is credited with saying that an ounce of prevention is worth a pound of cure. If people took godly premarital counseling seriously, they could reduce the need for crisis counseling later and perhaps reduce the incidence of divorce. Yet what is called premarital counseling is often little more than preceremonial counseling, because those involved are more concerned with who will stand where during the ceremony than where the new couple will stand in relationship to each other once they have begun life together. While premarital counseling is important for all couples, it is indispensable for those coming from broken or unstable homes, those who've been engaged before and had that engagement broken, and those on the rebound from another relationship.

If you, dear reader, are single because of death, divorce, separation, or choice, don't feel you must rush into a relationship. Let Jesus stabilize you first. Some fear they cannot be complete unless they are married. While this feeling is understandable, the reasoning is flawed. We must resist the urge to jump into a relationship before we are spiritually and emotionally healed and whole. One of the principles at the foundation of a healthy marriage contradicts the mathematical law that says 50 percent plus 50 percent makes 100 percent. To have a healthy marriage, each spouse must be willing to give 100 percent. Jesus put it another way. He said that when two people unite in marriage, one plus one makes one, not two.

So, the best way to handle divorce is to prevent it. But how is the church to relate to those who have divorced? And how should it relate to other singles?

The church and singles

Some people, some pastors included, are uncomfortable with the fact that single parents are attending their churches. "I don't want these divorced people in my church," one pastor said. "First thing you know, they'll be getting together, and then they'll want me to marry them. What am I going to do about Matthew 19? Let them go to someone else's church."

While admittedly, the church cannot encourage divorce, it is to be a gathering place for the wounded. It must not be a place where the members offer their love only to those who do what they want them to do.

People usually won't change the direction of their life until they hit bottom. Therefore, it is not surprising that many people do not turn to the Lord until their lives have come apart either through divorce or through the death of a spouse. But they don't always return to church immediately to seek healing. When people have been injured in an accident, they often must be stabilized before they're taken to an emergency room. The same principle applies when something emotionally traumatic occurs, like the breakup of a family or the death of a spouse.

It is important that we as members of the church family look for opportunities to minister to the singles, especially single-parent families. The phenomenon is not going to go away. The challenge that faces the church is to relate to single-parent families without seemingly giving the impression that its prevalence somehow makes it an acceptable option for people to choose deliberately.

In view of the challenge facing our families, our communities, and the church, how shall we relate to singles? First, we must receive those who come to us as singles. Second, we must minister to them according to the instructions given in the Word of God. And third, we must resist the pressure of contemporary society, which is seeking to convince us that the single-parent home is as desirable an option as the two-parent home comprised of a man and a woman.[2]

People can't prevent their marriage from eventually being dissolved by death, but they can apply the biblically based principles that reduce the risk of divorce. The church plays an important role as a center for teaching these principles. It should

- nourish existing families,
- call attention to the factors that damage marriages,
- minister to those who are single, and
- use all possible means to prevent the creation of one-parent families.

The church may accomplish these things by restating its commitment to the family and to the institution of marriage and by offering clear, biblical preaching and teaching.

However, the coin has two sides. If the body of Christ has a responsibility toward single people (whatever the reason they became single), single people also have a responsibility to the church. People who do not intend to try to live their lives according to the principles set forth in the Word of God should rethink their relationship to the church. We all fall short of the ideal in one way or another, but that's not the same as publicly professing commitment to the biblical ideal that the church proclaims when one has no intention of actually trying to base one's life on that ideal.

Single parents can take comfort in God's declaration that He is a father to the fatherless and a defender of the widows (Psalm 68:5). He says that He watches over the stranger and sustains the fatherless and the widow (Psalm 146:9). He may demolish the proud man's house, but He keeps the widow's boundaries intact (Proverbs 15:25).

When Jesus was walking among us, He said of Himself, "The Spirit of the Lord is upon me, because he hath anointed me to preach the gospel to the poor; he hath sent me to heal the brokenhearted, to preach deliverance to the captives, and recovering of sight to the blind, to set at liberty them that are bruised" (Luke 4:18). What a comfort to realize that He is willing to take charge of our lives whatever our home situations, and that if we will allow Him, the Holy Spirit will work to stabilize us emotionally and spiritually.

In the beginning, God saw that it was not good that Adam was alone. While single parenthood is a growing phenomenon in the twenty-first century, it is still not good that a man or a woman should be alone. Whatever our situation, though, we can find comfort in this promise of Jesus: "Behold, I am with you always."

Points to Ponder
1. Single-parent families in the church will continue to increase in numbers.
2. God said it was not good that a man or a woman be alone, yet sin and its consequences have damaged His plan.
3. While the church must accept and minister to single-parent families, it shouldn't encourage this arrangement as a substitute for traditional marriage.

4. Marriage is not a case where one-half plus one-half equals one, but rather where one plus one equals one.
5. The decision next in importance to that of accepting Jesus as our personal Savior is that of whom we will marry.

Homework Assignment
1. Whether you're single or married, make sure you don't allow roots of bitterness to grow in your life. Ask the Holy Spirit to give you the gift of forgiveness.
2. Singles should not be the only ones ministering to singles. Think of ways in which the entire church family can express their acceptance of singles.

---

1. *U.S. Statistical Abstract, 1980-1998,* table number 76.

2. See, e.g., the cover article of *Time* magazine for August 28, 2000: "Who Needs a Husband?" and "The New Single Mom—Why the Traditional Family Is Fading Fast," *Newsweek,* May 28, 2001.

CHAPTER
10

What's
in a Name?

"Therefore if any man be in Christ, he is a new creature: old things are passed away; behold, all things are become new."—the apostle Paul

The concepts expressed in this chapter may be difficult for the reader to appreciate at first—not because they're complicated but because they disagree with the conventional wisdom of the day. I respectfully request that you reserve judgment until you've reached the end of the chapter. I'm convinced there are two sides to every coin. The discussion here is by no means exhaustive, but it may give you some ideas to consider. The implications of the concepts suggested here for family relationships will be obvious.

The theory of personality types has been around since before the beginning of the Christian era, but the idea seems to have gained prominence during the past forty years or so. As a result, thousands of Christians have come to believe and teach the four temperaments as a means of understanding human nature and behavior.

The two most prominent promoters of this philosophy have been Tim LaHaye, most recently the coauthor of the enormously successful Left Behind series, and Florence Littauer, popular author and seminar presenter. Perhaps more than anyone else, these people can be credited with influencing millions to understand and explain themselves in terms of sanguine, choleric, melancholy, and phlegmatic.

The concept of the four temperaments has its roots with the Greek Empedocles, who developed the theory that there were four elements—earth, air, fire, and water—and that each element had its own god or god-

76

dess. Later, Hippocrates expanded the theory of four elements and taught that there were also four corresponding body fluids or humors: blood, yellow bile, black bile, and phlegm. He taught that the yearly seasons caused variations in these humors. Hippocrates believed that individuals have different proportions of the humors and that one of the humors is more or less dominant in each person. Still later, Plato, who had studied under Socrates, taught that the qualities of the elements and the constitution of the humors related directly to behavior. People also linked the four humors and the four elements with the zodiac.

During the Middle Ages, the alchemists—who believed that the human body, like all other material things, was composed of the four elements—thought that each individual had his or her own particular mixture. They called this mixture *temperamentum*. They believed that the influence of the constellations and planets determined each person's *temperamentum* at conception and birth and that the aptitudes, weaknesses, and chances of success or failure of all human beings sprang from their elemental composition.

The four temperaments today

Though some may find the idea of temperaments as taught in recent years harmless or even helpful, it is important that we consider not only their origins but also their implications for the Christian life. It is generally taught that each of the four temperaments have both positive traits and negative traits.

Personality Type	Positive Traits	Negative Traits
Sanguine	enjoying, optimistic, friendly	restless, weak-willed, emotionally unstable
Choleric	strong-willed, practical, a leader, optimistic	hot-tempered, cruel, impetuous, self-sufficient
Melancholy	sensitive, perfectionistic, analytical, faithful, self-sacrificing	self-centered, pessimistic, moody, revengeful
Phlegmatic	witty, dependable, practical, efficient	slow, lazy, a tease, stubborn, indecisive

Most people wouldn't mind being labeled a sanguine if by that means they're "enjoying," "optimistic," and "friendly." But they might be offended if being sanguine means they are "restless," "weak-willed," and "emotionally unstable." How would my spouse feel if, in the presence of others, I were to say that she is melancholy and by that I mean she is "self-centered," "pessimistic," "moody," and "revengeful"?

Notice that though the ancient Greeks and Romans promoted the idea of the four personality types, nowhere do we find in either the Old or New Testaments inspired references to them. In this regard, the authors of the book *Four Temperaments, Astrology and Personality Testing,* comment:

> Certainly, God created humanity with individual differences, but He did not create the four temperament categories. If the four temperaments theory of personality were biblical, such descriptive categories would have been developed in Scripture, at least to some degree. For instance, Scripture clearly delineates between the Gentiles and the Jews, between the saved and the lost, and between the flesh and the spirit. Such categories are not simply hinted at or creatively drawn out of a few verses. Chapters and entire books are devoted to distinguishing between believers and unbelievers and between walking after the flesh or according to the Spirit. Therefore, if there is to be another system for understanding the dynamics of personality and behavior, one would expect as clear a presentation in Scriptures, if indeed, it is one to be followed by Christians.[1]

What does labeling by personality have to do with the Christian life? Labeling implies that we were destined to be what we are and we can't help it. The gospel writers disagree. The apostle Peter declares that when people give their heart to Jesus, they are fundamentally changed:

> Grace unto you, and peace, be multiplied. Blessed be the God and Father of our Lord Jesus Christ, which according to

his abundant mercy hath begotten us again unto a lively hope by the resurrection of Jesus Christ from the dead, to an inheritance incorruptible, and undefiled, and that fadeth not away, reserved in heaven for you, who are kept by the power of God through faith unto salvation ready to be revealed in the last time (1 Peter 1:2-5).

The gospel is not a reformed extension of the old life, nor even a new life built on the old. Rather, it is an entirely new beginning. Doubtless, we are unique as individuals, but it is not consistent with Scripture to teach that what we are, we must remain. The gospel is about change. The purpose of the gospel is to bring our characters into conformity to the character of Jesus.

A close look at the positive and negative traits of the four temperaments reveals that there is among them a mixture of personality (who I am) with character (what I am). At what point are the negative traits of temperament really flaws of character? Another question: If everyone can be characterized by one or two of the temperaments, then which temperaments would we say Jesus had?

While those who teach the four temperaments don't intend to promote this kind of thinking, the four-temperaments theory can easily become an excuse for negative behavior. "I was born that way; that's my temperament. Therefore, I can't help the way I am." Scripture blames our faults on something else. It declares that the human heart "is deceitful above all things, and desperately wicked: who can know it?" (Jeremiah 17:9). Could it be that we run the risk of frustrating the work of the gospel in our lives by labeling ourselves with designations originated by pagans using the fallen human condition as the baseline?

What might the apostle Paul say to us if we tried to explain to him why we find no harm in the temperaments? Might not he say the following?

As ye have therefore received Christ Jesus the Lord, so walk ye in him: rooted and built up in him, and stablished in the faith, as ye have been taught, abounding therein with thanksgiving. Beware lest any man spoil you through philosophy and vain deceit, after the tradition of men, after the rudiments of the world, and not after Christ. For in him dwelleth all the fullness of the Godhead bodily. And ye are complete in him, which is the head of all principality and power (Colossians 2:6-10).

Freudian determinism?

The Freudian concept of determinism—which is, basically, that we must remain what we are—has strongly influenced contemporary philosophy. The Bible doesn't deny what we are, but it sets before us the option of a new beginning: "Therefore if any man be in Christ, he is a new creature: old things are passed away; behold, all things are become new" (2 Corinthians 5:17). Again, we read in 1 Corinthians 6:9-11:

Know ye not that the unrighteous shall not inherit the kingdom of God? Be not deceived: neither fornicators, nor idolaters, nor adulterers, nor effeminate, nor abusers of themselves with mankind, nor thieves, nor covetous, nor drunkards, nor revilers, nor extortioners, shall inherit the kingdom of God. And such were some of you: but ye are washed, but ye are sanctified, but ye are justified in the name of the Lord Jesus, and by the Spirit of our God.

Again, Paul writes:

But ye are washed, but ye are sanctified, but ye are justified in the name of the Lord Jesus, and by the Spirit of our God (1 Corinthians 6:11).

Beloved, now are we the sons of God, and it doth not yet appear what we shall be: but we know that, when he shall appear, we shall be like him; for we shall see him as he is (1 John 3:2).

As many as are led by the Spirit of God, they are the sons of God (Romans 8:14).

The earnest expectation of the creature waiteth for the manifestation of the sons of God (Romans 8:19).

Ye may be blameless and harmless, the sons of God, without rebuke, in the midst of a crooked and perverse nation, among whom ye shine as lights in the world (Philippians 2:15).

A focus on temperaments puts self, not Christ, as its center. God did not intend the Christian life to be a study of human personality and temperaments, but rather a process in which Christ and His character are the on-going focus of our attention. An emphasis on temperaments can easily become a spiritual self-help program in which people try to pull themselves up by their own bootstraps. The Christian life, in contrast, is based on a very personal relationship with Jesus Christ. It is not a system of formulas or a collection of humanly devised means for self-improvement.

Formerly, people were valued for their character. They considered character development important. Now the emphasis seems to be on personality and image. To complicate things further, a focus on personality types runs the risk of frustrating God's plan for our lives as revealed in Ephesians 3:19, which holds before Christians the wonderful possibility of being "filled with all the fullness of God." Which would you choose: to "be filled with all the fullness of God" or to discover that you're sanguine?

How does the fruit of the Spirit as enumerated in Galatians 5:22, 23 relate to the personality types? "The fruit of the Spirit is love, joy, peace, longsuffering, gentleness, goodness, faith, meekness, temperance." And where do the characteristics of love that Paul gave in 1 Corinthians 13 fit in the personality-type scheme of things? True love is kind, not jealous or proud. It is not selfish and doesn't have a temper. It is longsuffering, patient, and optimistic.

The apostle Peter wrote:

Beside this, giving all diligence, add to your faith virtue; and to virtue knowledge; and to knowledge temperance; and to temperance patience; and to patience godliness; and to godliness brotherly kindness; and to brotherly kindness charity. For if these things be in you, and abound, they make you that ye shall neither be barren nor unfruitful in the knowledge of our Lord Jesus Christ (2 Peter 1:5-8).

Notice that the Lord didn't inspire Peter to say, "Add virtues to your temperament strengths."

As Christians, God has called us to measure ourselves by the fruit of the spirit, the characteristics of true love, the Sermon on the Mount, Philippians 4:8, and the Ten Commandments. We are safer measuring ourselves by the standard of the character of Jesus Christ than by the four temperaments, whose origin is distinctly pagan and whose baseline is fallen human nature.

A young camel was having a conversation with its mother. "Mother, why do we have big bumps on our backs?"

"Honey, the humps on our backs allows us to store lots of water so we can travel through the desert."

"OK, Mom, but why do we have such big, funny feet?"

"Sweetheart, our feet are shaped this way so we can walk across the sand without sinking into it."

"Why do we have such long eyelashes?"

"So we can keep the sand out of our eyes when there's a terrible sandstorm."

"Mother, if we're made for the desert, then what are we doing here in this zoo?"

The popular view is that we must remain what we are. But God never meant for us to be confined in the zoo of our past, whether by inheritance or environment. The gospel intends for us to have a new start, to press on toward the mark for the prize of the high calling of God in Christ Jesus.

Perhaps we have inadvertently mixed truth with error, the sacred with the profane. The good news is that, in Christ, God has given us all the help we need in order to overcome in this dark world. We mustn't allow ourselves to be locked in a zoo of worldly perspectives and philosophy. In making us His sons and daughters in Christ, God has made us for greater things.

It is becoming more and more common for people to take concepts of the world and, in effect, to try to "Bible-ize" them. We must resist the tendency to test the truth of the Bible by the yardstick of science or pagan philosophers. On the contrary, we must test everything else by the Word of God. Though it has been said that all truth is God's truth, we must be careful with this concept. When truth is mixed with error, it becomes corrupted, and to the extent that it contains error, it is no longer true.

In the short run at least, error is stronger than truth. I say this because when people mix error with truth, the error gains credibility; yet when truth is mixed with error, the truth tends to be washed out. This is why Scripture teaches that darkness and light have no fellowship with each other: "What fellowship hath righteousness with unrighteousness? and what communion hath light with darkness?" (2 Corinthians 6:14).

Though we recognize that each member of the family is unique, our focus should not be on who has what personality type but rather on the common goal, which is to grow in grace (2 Peter 3:18) and to develop characters that are compatible with our high calling as members of the heavenly family.

What's in a name? The answer is "Much." In Bible times and in many cultures even today, a name indicates the type of person we are. We must resist the temptation to label others and ourselves. Rather than institutionalizing our weaknesses, as Christians, we'll appreciate our potential in Christ. Our focus will not be on self but on Him.

I close this chapter with a text that identifies both who we are and who we must become: "Beloved, [this is speaking to us as families], now are we the sons [and daughters] of God, and it doth not yet appear what we shall be: but we know that, when he shall appear, we shall be like him; for we shall see him as he is" (1 John 3:2).

Points to Ponder
1. We must be on guard lest a focus on temperaments: (a) causes us to accept negative character traits as simply a matter of who we are, (b) leads us to think that, inasmuch as we are the way we are, that is the way we must stay, and (c) causes us to attempt to change ourselves rather than die to self and allow the Holy Spirit to change us into the image of Christ.
2. God has called Christians to focus on developing their characters, not their personalities. The Holy Spirit must drive true character development.

3. The fruit of the Spirit and the spirit of true love as outlined in 1 Corinthians 13 will give us the ability to relate in a Christlike manner to those around us.
4. A self-improvement program that doesn't require Jesus in the life is not genuine and will ultimately fail.

Homework Assignment
1. List the characteristics of love as enumerated in 1 Corinthians 13.
2. Note the characteristics of love in your list that you feel you need to emphasize in your own life as you relate to the other members of your family.

Recommended Reading
Four Temperaments: Astrology & Personality Testing, by Martin and Deirdre Bobgan, is an interesting book on the subject of personality types.

---

1. Martin and Deirdre Bobgan, *Four Temperaments: Astrology & Personality Testing* (Santa Barbara, Calif.: EastGate Publishers, 1992), 70.

CHAPTER
11

Big Boys
Do Cry

*"Lofty mountains are full of springs; great hearts
are full of tears."*–Joseph Roux, 1834–1886

A man asked his friend how he was feeling. The friend replied,
"You know how you feel when you're leaning back in a chair and you
lose your balance and then catch yourself at the last second?"

"Yes."

"Well, I feel that way all the time!"

Feelings are . . . how can I explain them? Let me try this definition.
Feelings are the way we feel. Just as we are in touch with our body
through sensations of hot and cold, pain and pleasure, so we are in
touch with the psychological and spiritual components of our life
through our emotions. There are many feelings: anger, happiness, fear,
compassion, grief, joy, security, and insecurity, to name just a few. In
the family setting, feelings are important because the atmosphere of
the home at any particular time is the sum of the feelings of its members.

The first thing we did when we were born was to cry. And until
we learned to talk, we communicated our needs primarily through
tears. Some babies communicate their needs this way more than others do!

As the years pass, little girls are taught that it's all right for them
to cry when they feel the need. Often, however, little boys are taught
that they're not supposed to cry. I remember how proud I felt when
finally I could fall off my bike or hit my finger with a hammer and

not cry. I thought this a good thing because the common wisdom of the day was that boys who cried were "cry babies." When serious things happen to a woman, she's inclined to tell others about them. When serious things happen to men, they try to hide it. They say "I don't want to talk about it." Since men also need to express emotion yet are not supposed to cry, they're apt to become angry and abusive. Not surprisingly, many people consider this behavior to be manly.

Fortunately for us and for our families, men cry more openly these days than we did thirty or forty years ago. This change hasn't occurred because we've become sissies but because society now allows us to be more sensitive. We're beginning to learn that we don't have to hide how we feel. General Schwartzkopf, the commanding general for the allies during Desert Storm, once confided to Barbara Walters his belief that a man who couldn't cry shouldn't lead men into battle.

Tears can express all the emotions, often at their deepest level. While some equate tears only with sadness, they also express life's deepest and most profound joy and happiness. It isn't unusual to see tears of joy in the eyes of a bride as she stands next to her beloved or to see tears well up in the eyes of a young father as he holds his newborn in his arms for the first time. And watching the Olympics, one often sees tears on the cheeks of the winners as the officials place the gold medals around their necks.

Weeping is also biblical. Ecclesiastes 3:4 says there is a season for everything, including a time to weep. Some of the greatest men of all time wept, among them the prophet Jeremiah (Jeremiah 14:17), Job (Job 16:20), David (Psalm 6:6), and Paul (Acts 20:19, 31). Scripture records of the most important Person who ever lived that He "offered up prayers and supplications with strong crying and tears unto him that was able to save him from death, and was heard in that he feared" (Hebrews 5:7).

Although some aspects of contemporary culture concern me, I appreciate the trend that encourages men to be kinder and gentler. As the hearts of fathers and mothers are turned to the children and the children to their parents, tears will be an important expression of emotion, both of sadness and of joy. We no longer need to heed the lesson that we were taught for so many years, that we must "keep a stiff upper lip."

Culture shock

When I was twenty-six, I took my wife and three small children to Pakistan. That's when I had my first really big encounter with my feelings during my adult years. I'll never forget the awe I felt as the ship that carried us pulled up to the dock in the port of Karachi. It was almost an out-of-body experience. For my first few months there, I felt as though I were in some giant theme park. But soon reality set in, and I developed a full-blown case of culture shock. People don't realize how thoroughly they are tied to their culture until they leave it. I became so stressed that after a while I actually wished I would have a nervous breakdown so I'd be sent home for "medical reasons." That would look so much better than leaving voluntarily and being considered a quitter!

The man who was president of the Pakistan Union at that time had been in Southern Asia for more than thirty years and was over that hump. He tried to encourage me. He would tell me that it was all in my mind and that I would soon feel better. He was right when he said the problem was in my mind, but that didn't make it any less painful. Though his intentions were admirable, his approach didn't do me any good. I was hurting, and I didn't want to hear it was all in my head. I didn't even want to hear I would soon feel better. What I wanted was some good, old-fashioned sympathy!

Looking back on my life, I wonder how many times I've told people, "You shouldn't feel that way," "You'll get over it," or "You'll just have to get used to it." Though I, too, was well-meaning, I can see now that I was just repeating history. It has taken time for me to learn that when people are hurting, they need to be comforted before they can be encouraged.

In the context of family, we must be careful not to attack each other's feelings. Telling people they shouldn't feel a certain way is counterproductive. It would be much kinder to acknowledge their feelings. Conditions produce feelings. The way to change feelings is not to hide them or reject them, but to seek to modify the conditions that cause them.

One day when I came home from work, I noticed that my wife was sitting on the couch in the family room. I said Hello as I walked past on my way to the study and then did an immediate about-face because I noticed that she looked as though she'd been crying. "What's the matter?" I asked.

"Baby Cakes died," she replied softly, without looking up.

Baby Cakes was our parakeet. He could say "My name is Baby Cakes," "I'm a silly bird," and "Happy Sabbath." We bought him when our granddaughter was a little girl and lived with us, and he was a part of our family. However, Baby Cakes hadn't been himself for the past month or so. He'd try to bite us when we put our hand in his cage, and he had stopped talking.

On hearing the sad news, I immediately went to my computer and then to the Internet. I clicked on www.Google.com and typed in the words, "Parakeet lifespan." At the speed of light, the search engine examined all the knowledge on the Internet regarding the lifespan of parakeets. Less than five minutes later, I called out to Betty, "How old was Baby Cakes?"

Back came the answer, "Nine years old."

Then came my comforting retort, "It says here that a parakeet's life expectancy is eight and a half years."

How was that for a sensitive, compassionate reply? Did I really think I was helping my wife feel better? The message she received from me amounted to, "Wipe away those tears and be thankful the bird lived six months longer than he was supposed to."

At this time of my life, I'm learning a lot about feelings. I'm learning some things I wish I had known many years ago. They would have gone a long way toward making things better for my family. People say confession is good for the soul, so let me tell you another tearjerker that helped to teach me the value of respecting other people's feelings. My family cried then. I'm crying now.

For several years we lived in the Pacific Northwest. I was teaching at Auburn Academy, near Seattle, which was nearly three thousand miles from our relatives in Florida. Driving across the country with four small children was a major undertaking. We had to spend several nights in motels along the way.

On one of our trips back home, we pulled away from a motel in the early morning. We hadn't gone five miles when one of the children began to cry. Through his tears he explained that he'd set his teddy bear on top of the car. As he cried, the rest of the family urged me to go back and try to find the toy, which must have fallen off almost immediately.

Looking back now, I can hardly believe what I did—or, I should say, what I didn't do. I mumbled something about being in a hurry to get where we were going and that we probably wouldn't find the teddy bear anyway. I felt I had to take a hard line and be tough, so I steeled myself against the tears and pleading.

I would give anything to be able to remake that decision. This time I would respect the feelings of my children and go back to look for the teddy. How glad I am that God is not like me. He is merciful, gracious, longsuffering, and abundant in goodness and truth. Oh, that is what I want to be like!

Tears for our parents

In the past few years, my wife and I have watched our parents grow old and pass to their rest. My parents lived some distance away during their last years, and I didn't see them very often. But my mother-in-law lived very close, and we did see a lot of her. Toward the end, my wife and her sisters took turns caring for her—she was suffering from dementia. At first they cried a lot. Later, when they would share with each other some of the things she did or said, they could smile—not because it was funny but as their way of coping. It's heartbreaking when your mother asks you every five minutes how many children you have.

As difficult as this experience was, it taught me something. I'm a problem solver. (They say most men are.) However, I'm learning there are problems that no one can solve, and sometimes all I can do is to be there. I'm learning that I don't always need to put in my two-cents' worth. I had to learn as a brother-in-law to stand back and let the sisters work together to confront the challenges in the last year of Mom's life. I'm thankful to say that, through the sadness of seeing our dear ones grow old and pass on, our extended family has drawn closer together than we were before.

These days, people encourage those who are passing through a personal crisis to find a support group. I believe in support groups. During a desperate time in my life, I found Al-Anon particularly helpful. I appreciate the support I received there. But when family is functioning correctly, no one understands quite like family members do.

People who work in a business setting frequently refer to their fellow employees as the "office family." We call the people at church our "church family," which is very special because it is a fellowship of faith. But we must not forget the most important family of all, the family at home. Scripture says that during the last days a message will go forth that will prepare people for the end-time events, and this message is for families. Not for office families or our golf buddies or even our support group. It is a message for husbands and wives, for parents and children, in the site of the most important of human relationships—the home.

Our homes need to be places where the family members can know they'll be understood and comforted when they're hurting. Big boys do—and should—cry. Someone has well said that tears are a language God understands. We need to stop telling others "You shouldn't feel that way" and learn to say "I'm sorry. How can I help?" Spouses and parents should put away words like "I don't want to talk about that" and stop giving the cold, silent treatment. Rather, they should say "This must be very hard for you. Do you want to talk about it?"

One day, Jesus went to the synagogue where He had grown up. When they asked Him to read the Scripture for the day, He chose Isaiah 61:1, 2: "The Spirit of the Lord God is upon me; because the Lord hath anointed me to preach good tidings unto the meek; he hath sent me to bind up the brokenhearted, to proclaim liberty to the captives, and the opening of the prison to them that are bound; to proclaim the acceptable year of the Lord, and the day of vengeance of our God; to comfort all that mourn."

These verses describe Jesus' calling—His destiny. I believe Jesus' calling should also be our calling in the end time. God calls us to bind up the brokenhearted, to comfort those who are sad. I've not always been the compassionate, sensitive husband and father that by God's grace I now want to become. How thankful we are that God's mercy is new every day. Ours should be too.

Big boys do cry. Sometimes crying is the most appropriate thing to do. Our tears can be like the tears we used to shed when we ran crying to mother for help. They can be tears of compassion, tears of sympathy for the hurts of others, or tears of joy and relief. Forgetting the tough-minded, insensitive things we may have done in the past, we can now press on toward the mark for the prize of the high calling of God in Christ Jesus our Lord, claiming the promise that he who goes forth and weeps, bearing precious seed, shall doubtless come again with rejoicing, bringing his sheaves with him (Psalm 126:6).

Two Prayers

Last night my little boy confessed to me
Some childish wrong;
And kneeling at my knee,
He prayed with tears—
"Dear God, make me a man
Like daddy—wise and strong;
I know you can."

Then while he slept
I knelt beside his bed,
Confessed my sins,
And prayed with a low-bowed head:
"O God, make me a child
Like my child here—
Pure, guileless,
Trusting Thee with faith sincere!"—*Andrew Gillies*

Points to Ponder

1. Although big boys do cry, they must not pout.
2. People can be strong and still shed tears. Jesus was strong, yet He

wept at the tomb of Lazarus.

3. Both men and women have emotions, but there are acceptable and unacceptable ways to express them.

4. Tears may be an expression of every emotion, from sadness to joy.

5. The Christian life should include the traits of empathy and compassion.

Homework Assignment

1. The next time a member of your family cries, instead of saying "Don't cry," or "It's going to be all right," try giving them a comforting hug.

2. The next time your spouse is upset, instead of trying to talk him (or her) out of his (or her) feelings, encourage him (or her) to express them.

CHAPTER
12

Sticks and Stones May Break My Bones

*" 'Sticks and stones may break my bones,'
but words will break our hearts."*–Robert Fulghum

When I was a student at Mount Vernon Academy, the boys who lived in the dormitory used to play a mean trick on each other. When several boys were visiting in a dorm room, inevitably, another boy would knock on the door. One of the boys in the room would quickly crawl under the bed, while the others would shout "Come on in."

The unsuspecting visitor would come in and sit down for a chat. In a minute or two, the ones who were in on the gag would turn the subject of the conversation to the buddy who was under the bed. They would begin to say negative things about him. Slowly but surely they would entice the unsuspecting visitor into the conversation. When the visitor would begin to say bad things about the one under the bed, out he would crawl. The visitor's face would turn beet red while the others would laugh uproariously.

Perhaps when you were a child and someone would begin to put you down, you would say a little ditty that went something like "Sticks and stones may break my bones, but words will never hurt me." Whoever made that one up must have been in denial big time, because, while a broken bone will eventually heal, ill-spoken words can do damage that lasts a lifetime. Few things affect family relationships more than the way we talk to each other.

Of all the gifts God has given us, the gift of speech is probably one of the most important and one of the most misused. This gift can literally be a blessing or a curse. James 3: 2-12 says,

> In many things we offend all. If any man offend not in word, the same is a perfect man, and able also to bridle the whole body. Behold, we put bits in the horses' mouths, that they may obey us; and we turn about their whole body. Behold also the ships, which though they be so great, and are driven of fierce winds, yet are they turned about with a very small helm, whithersoever the governor listeth.
>
> Even so the tongue is a little member, and boasteth great things. Behold, how great a matter a little fire kindleth! And the tongue is a fire, a world of iniquity: so is the tongue among our members, that it defileth the whole body, and setteth on fire the course of nature; and it is set on fire of hell. For every kind of beasts, and of birds, and of serpents, and of things in the sea, is tamed, and hath been tamed of mankind: but the tongue can no man tame; it is an unruly evil, full of deadly poison. Therewith bless we God, even the Father; and therewith curse we men, which are made after the similitude of God. Out of the same mouth proceedeth blessing and cursing.
>
> My brethren, these things ought not so to be. Doth a fountain send forth at the same place sweet water and bitter? Can the fig tree, my brethren, bear olive berries? either a vine, figs? so can no fountain both yield salt water and fresh.

The way we talk to one another affects even our profession of faith: "If anyone considers himself religious and yet does not keep a tight rein on his tongue, he deceives himself and his religion is worthless" (James 1:26, NIV).

Sins of the tongue

Most of us would have to admit that we often miss the mark in this important indicator of our religious profession. The Bible specifically identifies what might be called sins of the tongue. Some of these are:

- Angry talk: "I fear, lest, when I come, I shall not find you such as I would, and that I shall be found unto you such as ye would not: lest there be debates, envyings, wraths, strifes, backbitings, whisperings, swellings, tumults" (2 Corinthians 12:20).
- Boasting: "Men shall be lovers of their own selves, covetous, boasters, proud, blasphemers, disobedient to parents, unthankful, unholy" (2 Timothy 3:2).
- Blasphemy: "Of whom is Hymenaeus and Alexander; whom I have delivered unto Satan, that they may learn not to blaspheme" (1 Timothy 1:20).
- Coarse joking: "Neither filthiness, nor foolish talking, nor jesting" (Ephesians 5:4).
- Deception: "We are not as many, which corrupt the word of God" (2 Corinthians 2:17).
- Flattery: "Neither at any time used we flattering words" (1 Thessalonians 2:5).
- Godless chatter: "O Timothy, keep that which is committed to thy trust, avoiding profane and vain babblings" (1 Timothy 6:20).
- Gossip: "They learn to be idle, wandering about from house to house; and not only idle, but tattlers also and busybodies, speaking things which they ought not" (1 Timothy 5:13).
- Lying: "Lie not one to another, seeing that ye have put off the old man with his deeds" (Colossians 3:9).
- Obscenity: "Ye also put off all these; anger, wrath, malice, blasphemy, filthy communication out of your mouth" (Colossians 3:8).
- Quarreling: "Ye are yet carnal: for whereas there is among you envying, and strife, and divisions, are ye not carnal, and walk as men?" (1 Corinthians 3:3).
- Slander: "Let all bitterness, and wrath, and anger, and clamour, and evil speaking, be put away from you, with all malice" (Ephesians 4:31).

Jesus said that the words we speak are an accurate indication of the kind of people we are. "A good man out of the good treasure of his heart bringeth forth that which is good; and an evil man out of the evil treasure of his heart bringeth forth that which is evil: for of the abundance of the heart his mouth speaketh" (Luke 6:45). The bottom line, dear reader, is that if we are to have godly homes, we must learn to speak to each other in a godly manner. While none of us will ever speak ancient Aramaic with a Galilean accent as Jesus did, we can and must speak contemporary English or whatever language we speak with a Christian accent. Our words will follow us into the judgment and will be a witness either for us or against us. The Lord Himself warns, "Men will have to give account on the day of judgment for every care-less word they have spoken. For by your words you will be acquitted, and by your words you will be condemned" (Matthew 12:36, 37, NIV).

Here are two questions to consider. First, why are we so nice to people who are total strangers and so unkind to people we love? Second, how long would we last on the job if we talked to our boss the way we talk to our spouse or children? I directed the second question to a congregation one time, and a man answered from the audience, "Until I got the words out of my mouth." Sometimes when I meet a young couple about to get married or who are recently married, I give them a bit of counsel in just one short sentence: "Be kind to each other."

A positive question

What would our homes be like if we always spoke kindly to each other? I'm not suggesting that we would always agree or that the children would always obey. But what would happen if, in spite of the on-going challenges of family life, we always spoke kindly to each other?

It is disheartening to realize how our misuse of words affects relationships between spouses and between parents and children. Many easily fall into the habit of coming home and saying any mean thing. Someone once suggested I preach a sermon entitled, "Treat Your Wife Like a Dog." At first I didn't catch on. Then the person reminded me that we usually talk nicer to our pets than we do to each other. While the words from God's mouth created this planet and all that is in it, the words from our mouths can destroy our world and the relation-ships most precious to us. James was right when he wrote that the tongue can set fires that result in great conflagrations, producing un-happy and broken homes.

Often people excuse themselves by saying, "But they were only words." The book of Proverbs points out that "only words" can:

- Destroy neighbors: "An hypocrite with his mouth destroyeth his neighbour" (Proverbs 11:9).
- Pierce like a sword: "There is that speaketh like the piercings of a sword" (Proverbs 12:18).
- Stir up anger: "Grievous words stir up anger" (Proverbs 15:1).
- Crush the spirit: "A wholesome tongue is a tree of life: but perverseness therein is a breach in the spirit" (Proverbs 15:4).

While that is the bad news, the good news is that words can also heal:

- "The lips of the righteous feed many" (Proverbs 10:21).
- "The tongue of the wise is health" (Proverbs 12:18).
- "A soft answer turneth away wrath" (Proverbs 15:1).
- "Pleasant words are as an honeycomb, sweet to the soul, and health to the bones" (Proverbs 16:24).

A person can learn much from other cultures. Our family lived for five years in Latin America. One of the many things I appreciated about the believers there was their custom of saying a prayer whenever they got into their car to go somewhere. They asked God's protection even when they were just going shopping. In our family, we usually pray before starting a trip, but saying a special prayer for safety before we drive around town was new to me. I must say it makes a lot of sense. This custom gave me an idea. Before we get out of the car to go into the house when we arrive home after a day on the job, why not bow our head and ask God to help us speak kindly to those we love?

While I was conducting a week-long series of revival meetings in a church, I was a houseguest in the pastor's home. One evening during their family worship, he invited all the family members to tell the person next to them what they liked about him or her. We're more accustomed to hearing siblings tell what they don't like about each other. Hearing those boys express appreciation for each other was an inspiration I've never forgotten.

So, remember—while sticks and stones may break our bones, unkind words can break our hearts. One of the indications that the parents' hearts have turned to the children and the children's to the parents will be that we are careful how we talk to each other. I invite you to consider changing the atmosphere of your home by changing the way you talk to those you love. Avoid words that tend to hurt. Try saying instead, "Good job," "I'm sorry," "Please forgive me," and "I love you."

Points to Ponder
1. The gift of speech is one of the most important of all the gifts God has given us.
2. How we talk to each other affects the atmosphere of the home.
3. We are inclined to talk nicer to people we don't know than to people we love.
4. We should make as much effort to talk kindly to those we love as we do to people we don't know.
5. Jesus said we will be judged by the words we speak, because how we talk indicates what kind of people we are.

Homework Assignment
1. When you come home from work tomorrow, before you open the door to go into the house, bow your head and offer a little prayer: "Dear Lord, help me to be kind."
2. Try to determine the circumstances in which you are most likely to say unkind words. When those circumstances occur, say a little prayer. You will be pleased with the result.

CHAPTER
13

Now You See It, Now You Don't

"Our anger and annoyance are more detrimental to us than the things themselves which anger or annoy us."–Marcus Aurelius, A.D. 121–180

The details escape me now. I was nearing a tollbooth on a turnpike off-ramp. I wasn't trying to be rude, but I did cut in front of another car. I didn't think much about it until suddenly I became aware that the driver of the other car had pulled up beside me. I have never seen someone so furious as that man was that day. He was exhibiting a full-blown case of road rage.

A friend related to me how, one day on the way to the office, he inadvertently cut in front of a driver. Looking in the rearview mirror, he could hardly believe his eyes when the angry driver took a gun out of the glove compartment and pointed it at him. Thank God, he didn't pull the trigger. Another case of road rage.

Rage is not just something for the road. All too often it is something that happens at home. Nearly every day we hear of another case of spouse abuse. By the way, spouse abuse is not gender specific. Although men do much more damage than women, research has shown that women also abuse their husbands. Furthermore, children may be not only victims of abuse but also perpetrators against their siblings and even their parents.

This chapter is about anger. Its impact on families is obvious. Anger is related to violence, crime, spouse and child abuse, divorce, stormy relationships, poor working conditions, and poor health. While it could be said that anger in itself is not sin, it is definitely an entry event that can, and usually does, cause us to sin. As families, we must address the challenge. There may be reasons for anger, but for sons and daughters of God, there can be no excuse for it. Christians in the last days will need to confront the fires of anger, contain them, and, by the power of the Holy Spirit, put them out.

Generally speaking, there are two types of anger. One type of anger is what we might call divine anger or righteous indignation. The other type we will call carnal anger.

In contrast to carnal anger, God's anger is vigorous, intense, controlled, and consistent with His love and mercy. He is never surprised, shocked, or outraged. Jesus manifested divine anger when people were violating principle. Yet, when the worst offense of all was being committed against Him, He didn't become angry. Rather, He prayed "Father, forgive them; for they know not what they do" (Luke 23:34).

"The wrath of man worketh not the righteousness of God" (James 1:20). Because most human anger is irrational, if left unchecked, it will lead to sin. Righteous indignation won't. Righteous indignation is the anger we feel when we witness certain forms of injustice and wicked acts.

On a recent visit to Oklahoma, I went to see the Oklahoma City Memorial. Until 9/11, the destruction of the Murrah building was the single worst act of terrorism committed in the United States in recent history. I walked through the first large arch, over which is inscribed the time, "9:01 A.M." Where the building once stood is a green lawn with brass chairs mounted on lighted glass bricks, memorializing those who were killed in the blast. What had been the street in front of the building is now a reflecting pool. The large arch at the end of the reflecting pool is inscribed with the time, "9:03 A.M." The blast occurred at 9:02 A.M.

As I walked among the chairs, tears came to my eyes. My feeling was righteous anger, or, if you please, righteous indignation. I thought of what had happened there, and it occurred to me that one of the greatest demonstrations of God's love is the final punishment of unrepentant sinners. Their punishment will not be intended to teach them a lesson, because they will be forever gone. Rather, their punishment is for the sake of the saved. God's message to the saved is "I care about what happened to you." "Vengeance is mine; I will repay, saith the Lord" (Romans 12:19).

In contrast to carnal anger, righteous indignation can motivate us to become positively involved in opposing social or personal evils. Yet we must remember that God has not called us to do what it is only His place to do.

What carnal anger does

Carnal anger is inconsistent with the goals of the new life in Christ. In fact, it can halt or severely retard the work of the Holy Spirit in the life because

- anger is numbered among the works of the flesh, and those who persist in this lifestyle will not inherit the kingdom of God: "Now the works of the flesh are manifest, which are these; adultery, fornication, uncleanness, lasciviousness, idolatry, witchcraft, hatred, variance, emulations, wrath, strife, seditions, heresies, envyings, murders, drunkenness, revellings, and such like: of the which I tell you before, as I have also told you in time past, that they which do such things shall not inherit the kingdom of God" (Galatians 5:19-21).
- anger is related to foolishness: "Be not hasty in thy spirit to be angry: for anger resteth in the bosom of fools" (Ecclesiastes 7:9).
- anger grieves the Holy Spirit: "Grieve not the Holy Spirit of God, whereby ye are sealed unto the day of redemption. Let all bitterness, and wrath, and anger, and clamour, and evil speaking, be put away from you, with all malice" (Ephesians 4:30).
- anger is a violation of the Christian's code of conduct as a member of the body of Christ: "Put off all these; anger, wrath, malice, blasphemy, filthy communication out of your mouth" (Colossians 3:8).
- anger stands in the way of effective prayer: "I will therefore that men pray every where, lifting up holy hands, without wrath and doubting" (1 Timothy 2:8).
- anger is always accompanied by other sins: "An angry man stirreth up strife, and a furious man aboundeth in transgression" (Proverbs 29:22).

- anger promotes jealousy and cruelty: "Wrath is cruel, and anger is outrageous; but who is able to stand before envy?" (Proverbs 27:4).

President Calvin Coolidge was a man of few words. One Sunday when he returned from church, his wife asked him what the minister talked about. "Sin," he replied.

"What did he say about it?"

"He was against it."

If someone should ask you what the Bible's attitude is toward anger, you may simply say, "It is against it." Although countless things may make us angry and although we must confess that we have all been angry at one time or another, the Bible leaves no room for doubt that anger has no place in the Christian's life.

- "Cease from anger, and forsake wrath: fret not thyself in any wise to do evil" (Psalm 37:8).
- "A wise man feareth, and departeth from evil: but the fool rageth, and is confident. He that is soon angry dealeth foolishly: and a man of wicked devices is hated" (Proverbs 14:16, 17).
- "He that is slow to wrath is of great understanding: but he that is hasty of spirit exalteth folly" (Proverbs 14:29).
- "He that is slow to anger is better than the mighty; and he that ruleth his spirit than he that taketh a city" (Proverbs 16:32).
- "Be not hasty in thy spirit to be angry: for anger resteth in the bosom of fools" (Ecclesiastes 7:9).
- "Dearly beloved, avenge not yourselves, but rather give place unto wrath: for it is written, Vengeance is mine; I will repay, saith the Lord" (Romans 12:19).
- "Let all bitterness, and wrath, and anger, and clamour, and evil speaking, be put away from you, with all malice: And be ye kind one to another, tenderhearted, forgiving one another, even as God for Christ's sake hath forgiven you" (Ephesians 4:31, 32).
- "Put off all these; anger, wrath, malice, blasphemy, filthy communication out of your mouth" (Colossians 3:8).

- "Let every man be swift to hear, slow to speak, slow to wrath: for the wrath of man worketh not the righteousness of God" (James 1:19, 20).

At times anger may not be obvious but may remain dormant as a quiet, seething resentment or indignation at some large or small offense, real or imagined. Sometimes anger explodes into a rage that motivates retaliation: violence or even murder. Anger can result

- when there is unresolved bitterness and resentment.
- when people feel they were slighted—they didn't get something they deserved. Anger from unfulfilled expectations may be exhibited not only toward other people but also toward God— as in the case of Jonah, who became angry that God didn't destroy Nineveh.
- when pride is damaged or to boost a sagging ego.

Anger can inflict lasting hurt. Surveys have been conducted to determine the extent of anger in the general population. In one study,[1] the question was asked, "If you could secretly push a button and thereby eliminate any person with no repercussions to yourself, would you ever press that button?" Some 69 percent of men and 56 percent of women said Yes.

A study cited in *What's Good About Anger,* by Lynette Hoy and Ted Griffin, found that 23 percent of Americans openly express their anger, 39 percent say they hold it in or hide it, 24 percent say they walk away, 23 percent confess to having hit someone, and 17 percent admit they have destroyed someone's property out of anger.

We can "catch" anger like a bad cold. Proverbs 22:24 counsels, "Make no friendship with an angry man; and with a furious man thou shalt not go." Children often learn anger from their parents—who thus become negative role models.

People often use anger to control others. Temper tantrums are not limited to little children. Many a husband and wife have found that anger is one way to get what they want. A person who has a problem with anger may deny it, especially if it is a quiet, seething resentment. But we can know we have a problem with anger when

- people often tell us we need to calm down.
- we feel tense much of the time.
- people ask us not to yell or curse so much.
- loved ones keep saying that we are hurting them.

Anger's effects

Though anger is an emotion, it may cause physical effects that are both immediate and long term. An immediate physical result will be an adrenaline rush—the heart beats faster, the palms sweat, acid production in the stomach increases greatly, and we experience insomnia. Among the long-term effects of anger are headaches and gastrointestinal, skin, and emotional disorders, to name a few. Probably the most common companion of anger is depression, which may cause not only emotional problems but physical and spiritual problems as well.

Anger has a powerful effect on the family, because when we are angry, we usually hurt the people closest to us. This results in alienation, grief, and, in the case of domestic violence, physical and emotional pain.

Sometimes the effects of breaking God's laws can take a long time manifesting themselves. Fortunately, God has designed us so anger will cause immediate physical and spiritual changes. This is actually a blessing, because then we can take immediate steps to overcome it.

There is a present-day pop psychologist who asserts, "Don't get mad, get even." They say revenge is sweet. But the Word of God tells us that revenge is God's business. Not only that, experience teaches that revenge is not sweet and in the end will produce only bitterness.

Others will say it's not healthy to hold anger in—we should tell people off or, if not, at least bang on the wall. When I was a student, I worked as a plasterer. One day I was called to repair a hole that a student had punched in a dormitory wall. He was told he had to pay the cost of the repair.

As I worked, he stood by and watched. "Take your time," he said, grinning. "Money is relative." Someone standing nearby murmured wistfully, "I wish it were my relative!"

I hope the student learned sooner rather than later that anger can precipitate events that can't be fixed as easily as a hole in the wall.

Friend, we get serious when there are problems with the roof or the refrigerator or the car. In many Christian homes, the problem of anger is serious and if not addressed will have eternal consequences.

While we need to know how to deal with our own anger, we also need to know how to relate to other members of the family when they become angry. Here are some steps we can take when others are angry:

- Speak softly and slowly.
- Ask sincere questions. ("Why do you feel that way?" "Can you help me to understand what you are saying?")
- Listen closely to the individual to hear what he (or she) is saying beyond the words he (or she) is speaking.
- Have a servant attitude. ("What can I do to help solve the problem?")
- Confess wrongs you may have committed and ask for forgiveness.
- Ask the Lord to open the door of opportunity for you to do something good for the angry person. ("If thine enemy hunger, feed him; if he thirst, give him drink: for in so doing thou shalt heap coals of fire on his head"—Romans 12:20.)
- Pray for the person who is angry.

A friend shared the secret of how he deals with anger. He told me he used to get into a verbal fight with one particular individual every time they were together. With a smile, he said that the problem went away when he learned to pray silently for that person every time they were in each other's presence. My friend called this the "flash prayer." The gospel is powerful. Despite the challenges of life, we can have victory over carnal anger.

I have decided that the emotion of anger subjects me to having a conflict of interest. That is, when I become angry, I lose whatever moral high ground I might have had. At that point, who was right and who was wrong is no longer an issue.

What shall we do when we are confronted with the challenge of our own anger and the anger expressed by other members of the family? Why not start with Romans 12:18: "If it be possible, as much as lieth in you, live peaceably with all men [i.e., husbands, wives, and children]." An effective implementation is the text, "A soft answer turneth away wrath: but grievous words stir up anger" (Proverbs 15:1).

This chapter and the previous one are critical to the atmosphere of the home. Before you move on to the next chapter, I invite you to prayerfully review these two chapters again. Words and anger are inseparable, inasmuch as words express and stir up anger. I believe that, by the grace of God, we can do better on both counts.

Points to Ponder
1. We are more likely to exhibit carnal anger than righteous indignation.
2. Anger that is not righteous indignation is inconsistent with the goals of the Christian life and will erode home life.
3. Depression has been described as anger turned inward.
4. Through the gospel, we can have victory over anger.
5. Prayer puts out anger like water puts out fire.

Homework Assignment
1. Determine that no matter what the other members of your family do, you will make Romans 12:18 your motto. Why not tape it to the fridge?
2. Remember Proverbs 15:1, "A soft answer turneth away wrath." Next time a member of the family is upset, try it!

---

1. Reported in *Psychology Today* in 1983.

CHAPTER
14

Isn't Anyone Listening?

"Be swift to hear and slow to speak."
—the apostle James

You're walking down the hall at work and you meet a colleague. He asks, "How are you doing?"

"Not very well," you reply.

"Great!" he says as he passes. "Have a good day."

Hey! Isn't anyone listening?

They were in the way going up to Jerusalem; and Jesus went before them: and they were amazed; and as they followed, they were afraid. And he took again the twelve, and began to tell them what things should happen unto him, saying, Behold, we go up to Jerusalem; and the Son of man shall be delivered unto the chief priests, and unto the scribes; and they shall condemn him to death, and shall deliver him to the Gentiles: And they shall mock him, and shall scourge him, and shall spit upon him, and shall kill him: and the third day he shall rise again.

And James and John, the sons of Zebedee, come unto him, saying, Master, we would that thou shouldest do for us whatsoever we shall desire. And he said unto them, What would ye that I should do for you? They said unto him, Grant unto us that we may sit, one on thy right hand, and the other on thy left hand, in thy glory (Mark 10:32-37).

What's going on here? Didn't they hear what Jesus had just said?

She stood in the door of my study, my wife of more than forty years. I had been doing some work on the computer when she came to the door and started talking. I stopped what I was doing for a minute and tried to pay attention. I don't remember now what she was talking about, but I remember wishing she would hurry. To a man's way of thinking, women can make a short story last a long time. I don't know who did the counting, but it has been estimated that in any single day, women use approximately twice as many words as do men.

I tried to give the appearance that I was listening, but I was secretly hoping she would get to the point. That's the way we men are. "So what's the problem? Get to the point." Then it hit me, and I wondered, *What kind of person am I?* There stood my wife talking to me. She wasn't making some big announcement or asking me to do anything for her. She was merely sharing everyday happenings. *This woman was sharing her life with me, and here I was, wishing she would hurry up and let me get back to my computer!*

To men, sharing our lives with our wives usually translates into being physically intimate. This may not be the only mistake we men make in our marriages, but it is a big one. The more I think about it, the clearer it becomes that in a good marriage, listening is sometimes more important than other forms of intimacy. To truly care for someone is to be willing to stop, look, and listen to that person.

Many of us are better programmed to talk than to listen. When other people are talking, we're more likely to be thinking of what we plan to say when they finish than we are to be listening to what they're saying. This must have been the case that day when Jesus and His disciples were headed toward Jerusalem. The atmosphere of our homes would be entirely different if we would implement James 1:19, "Wherefore, my beloved brethren [and sisters], let every man [woman and child] be swift to hear, slow to speak."

A number of years ago I received an invitation to be the chaplain of a mission hospital. At that time, hospital chaplaincy was a developing profession. The training included watching an autopsy and a surgery (during which, I blush to admit, I fainted). But most importantly, the emphasis was on how to listen. We can never know what people are thinking and how they feel unless we give them a chance to express their thoughts and feelings.

All families need to learn some of the skills of chaplaincy. Gayle Peterson, a family therapist, teaches that the way in which a family makes decisions is often more crucial to positive feelings between family members than what decisions they make. More often than not, relationships are defined by feelings; and we'll never know how other members of the family feel unless we're willing to listen.

I'm more inclined to want to tell others what I think than to listen to their point of view. It's like the old saw says, "My mind is made up; don't confuse me with the facts." The wise man had an answer for that one, "He that answereth a matter before he heareth it, it is folly and shame unto him" (Proverbs 18:13). As spouses and parents, our penchant to lecture, scold, judge, and nag will be greatly diminished when we encourage all the members of the family to express their feelings.

Focus on their interests

Do you sometimes feel that when you do try to communicate with your children, they respond with little more than Yes and No answers? One day I was trying to strike up a conversation with my grandson, and all he was saying was Yes and No. Suddenly it occurred to me that, in trying to get him involved in the conversation, I was, in effect, interrogating him. Most of the questions I was asking required only Yes and No answers. I was expecting him to fill in the details, but he wasn't doing that.

I decided to risk a moment of silence. When the boy realized no more questions were coming, he began to talk nonstop! And he talked about the things that interested him. Looking back, I can see that the problem had been not only the kind of questions I was asking but also the topic—I had been asking him about things that interested me. He was polite and answered my questions. But the conversation really took off when I became willing to listen to what interested him.

Have you noticed that God does more listening than He does talking? This is especially true when strong feelings and anger are involved.

When one member of the family becomes angry, the others tend to take sides. At that point, any possibility of listening objectively goes out the window.

Let's set up a typical scenario and do a case study. Our teenager comes home from school upset. She yells at us and is unpleasant with everyone and everything. Now, we have some options. We can yell back at her, we can ignore her, or we can listen to her.

To be good listeners, we must have self-control, especially when the other person has just insulted us or otherwise made us angry. In the case of our children, we must remember that their willingness to talk to us is the main vehicle through which we can bring change to their lives, and yelling at them definitely doesn't encourage communication.

It becomes next to impossible to continue an argument if one of those involved pulls his or her own feelings out of the equation and assumes the role of listener. Stepping outside the argument provides another benefit. Listening implies caring. If we will choose to assume the role of listener, we will not be so likely to hear the oft-repeated complaint, "All you ever do is criticize me!"

Someone once confided to me that she paid a counselor eighty dollars an hour merely to listen to her. She cried as she added, "I don't have anyone to talk to." Of course, we could always talk to ourselves, but that is not the way God made us. When God said it was not good that Adam should be alone, He wasn't talking only about marriage. To be healthy emotionally and spiritually, we all need to have someone who will listen to us. Planes would fly into each other if pilots couldn't talk with the tower. Many families have fallen apart for lack of being able to communicate effectively with each other.

These days, support groups have developed to help people with nearly every kind of need. People appreciate these groups because they comprise a gathering of people who understand what each other is going through and who will listen. God made the family to be the original support group. If the members of the family learn how to listen to each other, the effect will be felt not only within the family but outside as well.

But beware! To be good listeners, we must be willing to give of our time. To listen effectively means something else too. It means that for the moment we will intentionally clear our minds of our own plans, dreams, schemes, and anxieties. In other words, to be good listeners, we have to manage what goes on in our own minds.

And good listeners aren't just silent receptacles, passively receiving the thoughts and feelings of others. Effective listeners respond with verbal and nonverbal cues that let the speaker know that they are listening and understanding. These responses are called feedback. They can be either verbal or body language. Body language that says "I'm listening" includes making eye contact, nodding the head, and leaning toward the speaker. Verbal feedback can include restating thoughts, such as "You say you couldn't remember where you put the keys?" or simple "Uh-huhs" that let the speaker know you're listening.

The adults in every home should encourage the art of listening. They could almost make it a game. Some rules for good listening that we can share and practice with our family members are:

- Be attentive but relaxed.
- Keep an open mind.
- Don't interrupt and impose your own solutions.
- Wait for the one speaking to pause before asking clarifying questions.
- Avoid questions that disrupt the speaker's train of thought.
- Try to feel what the other person is feeling.

It is difficult to be good listeners when the person who is talking (or shouting) to us is clearly upset. To keep ourselves from becoming upset, we can encourage them to express their feelings. Responses that help to defuse the situation include:

- "I see."
- "I understand."
- "That's a good point."
- "I can see that you feel strongly about that."
- "I can understand how you could see it like that."

Though some people are born listeners, most of us aren't. Many times in my ministry people have called and said, "Pastor, I would like to come over and talk with you. I need some advice." When someone made this request, my tendency was to focus more on the "I need some advice" (which is actually, "I need someone who will listen to me") than on the "I want to talk to you." Experience teaches that often we can be more effective by simply listening than by giving advice. At the end of the day, each of us must own our own problems. Other people can't solve our problems for us. So, what we need most is someone who will listen to us in such a way that we can see all our options clearly, because in the final analysis, we must choose what we will do. That's true, too, of those who need us to listen to them.

Listening to children

We parents and grandparents owe it to our children to be good listeners and by so doing to teach them to be good listeners. Here are three points to bear in mind when listening to children:

1. We should encourage them to talk. Some children (though not all of them!) need an invitation to start talking. A question like "What did you do in school today?" is more difficult for a child to answer than "What did you do in school today that you really liked?"

2. We must listen patiently. People think faster than they speak. And children, with both a limited vocabulary and limited experience in talking, often take longer than adults to find the right words. During a meal our family was enjoying together, I was talking with one of my grandchildren, asking her some questions. As she would begin to answer in a child-like manner, one of the adults at the table would break in with "What she means is . . ." and then an explanation. I finally had to say, "Let the child tell us what she means."

3. We should hear them out. Often, parents will cut off their children before they've finished speaking. We're tempted to form an opinion or reject the child's point of view before

the child has finished communicating his or her thought. When listening to children, we must be as respectful as we would be to any other person.

Earlier, I mentioned that we should ask questions that encourage interaction and not dead-end Yes and No answers. But it is also important that we recognize that a child's attention span is not as long as ours, so it's helpful to recognize when it's time to end a conversation.

We often have more interaction with the people at work or at school than we do with those we love at home. As the Holy Spirit turns the hearts of the parents to their children and the children to their parents, the home will become a place where we know there are people who really understand us and who will listen to us when we become upset without becoming upset themselves.

One day I received a phone call from one of my sons. He and his family live only a few miles from us, but he calls nearly every day to "check in." We small-talked for a few minutes, and then somehow the conversation turned toward spiritual things. My son began to ask questions—not questions of faith but of doubt, such as how we know that Christianity is the only true religion.

In the past, these kinds of questions would have elicited a sermon from me or at least a defensive "you should know better than that" attitude. But as he talked, I made the intentional decision to listen and react to him as though he were a person sitting next to me on an airplane whom I had never met before. For at least five minutes he expressed doubts he was having at the moment. Suddenly he stopped talking and said, "Dad, thank you for listening to me. I thought if I talked this way to you, you would really go after me." I'm thankful that as we grow older we can, with experience, become smarter!

Usually these days, trial and error in our family relationships results in error. Our only sure guide must be Scripture, which even in the twenty-first century is still profitable for doctrine, for reproof, for correction, and for instruction in righteousness. It will show us how to get along with those we love.

Yes, when all is said and done, our family should be our favorite support group. It can be when we, as parents and children (that's everyone, because we're each someone's child), become swift to hear and slow to speak. When we are, it will follow that we will be "slow to wrath" (James 1:19).

Points to Ponder
1. God listens to us more than He talks to us.
2. We should be quick to hear and slow to speak.
3. Sharing our lives with our loved ones means being willing to listen to them.
4. Families fall apart when the family members don't communicate with each other. We can't communicate with each other when no one is listening.
5. We should be more willing to listen than to give advice.

Homework Assignment
1. The next time a loved one is talking to you, stop what you are doing and look at him or her (except when you're driving a car). The point of this exercise will be to learn to give those who are speaking to us our undivided attention.
2. The next time someone asks you for advice, see if you can, by gently asking questions, help that person come to his or her own conclusions.

CHAPTER
15

McDonalds, What Have You Done to Us?

"Health is better than wealth."—John Ray, 1628-1705

Some things have snob appeal; some things don't. Occasionally, when I hear of some accomplishment, I think to myself, "I wish I could do that." Well, what I am about to tell you about myself doesn't have snob appeal. I can't image anyone wishing they could do it too.

I eat rat poison every day. Now mind you, the label on the bottle doesn't say "Rat Poison." It says "Warfarin." But the first time I used Warfarin, I was trying to kill rats. This chemical thins the blood. It degrades the blood's clotting ability and causes massive internal hemorrhaging.

I guess I owe you an explanation. When I was still a teenager, a doctor noticed that I have an irregular heartbeat. He was taking my pulse during a routine check-up and found the beats difficult to count. After taking various tests, I was diagnosed with atrial fibrillation. In addition to the sino-atrial node, which is the heart's natural pacemaker, I have other volunteer cells trying to establish their rhythm. As a result, the atria are pumping along at 130 to 140 beats per minute.

It wasn't until I was in my fifties that I consented to have a complete workup of my heart. Until then I had lived a normal life. I didn't feel my condition posed any real problem. I didn't pay attention to the extra beats and otherwise felt normal.

However, this condition can cause a complication. When the atria are contracting at that speed, they can't empty themselves completely.

The pooling of the blood could allow a clot to form. I probably don't need to tell you that clots can cause strokes.

The cardiologist told me that if I did nothing, at my age I had a one percent chance per year of having a stroke. He suggested that I take a blood thinner. He said taking an aspirin a day wouldn't be sufficient in my case.

The idea of taking rat poison grosses me out. In addition, it's both a nuisance and an expense—besides the cost of the medication, I have to get my blood tested every month to make sure it's not too thin or too thick. Too much Warfarin could cause an internal hemorrhage. The cure could be as bad as the disease!

So why not just take an aspirin every day anyway, or do nothing and take my chances? One percent doesn't sound like much of a risk.

I'll tell you why I decided to follow the doctor's advice. I made that choice because if I were to have a stroke, it wouldn't ruin just my life. Who would have to call 911, and, if I survive, who would push me around in a wheelchair, bathe me, and all the rest? My wife.

Some may say, "It's my life; I can live it the way I want." However, that's absolutely false. Long ago I realized that my health doesn't belong to me alone. It belongs to my entire family. If I love those who love me, I can't live it any old way I want. What happens to my health happens to my entire family.

Fast-food lifestyle

So, we ought to live a healthy lifestyle to avoid becoming a burden to our family. But there's another reason for paying attention to health. While there can be no doubt that the most important thing a parent should try to instill in a child is faith in God, a close second would be a healthy lifestyle. From the very first moments of life, parents play a key role in the nutrition and overall well-being of their children. They teach the children how to care for their body; they set the example the children will follow; and they set in them the habits of living that will become either a blessing or a curse to the children in later life.

Unfortunately, between 16 and 33 percent of children and adolescents in the United States are obese. More than three hundred thousand deaths per year result from unhealthy weight gain, which is due to poor diet and lack of exercise.[1] We can trace a direct line from this increase in obesity to the amount of fast food consumed. Fast food has surpassed religion as the opiate of the masses. In 1970, some $6 billion dollars was spent on fast food. In the year 2000, the amount was $110 billion dollars.

McDonalds, what have you done to us?

Is it fair to lay obesity and its consequences at the doorstep of the fast-food industry? Though some say Yes and have even tried to take the companies to court, I say No. The problem is that this generation refuses to take responsibility for its own decisions. Tufts University's national studies show that more than 80 percent of parents consider eating dinner with their children very important. However, less than 50 percent actually sit down together on a daily basis. And the number who do decreases as the children get older. In a study that involved more than sixteen thousand children, Harvard Medical School has documented that only 43 percent of American children eat dinner daily with members of their family. More than half of the nine-year-olds eat family dinners, but only about one-third of the fourteen-year-olds do.

There used to be something special about breaking bread together. If it can be said that families that pray together stay together, it can also be said that eating together helps bring about the same result. When parents and children eat together and enjoy each other's company, they're fostering a sense of belonging and mutual trust. Eating together as a family not only provides opportunity for adults to model table manners and nutritious food choices, but it also encourages adult/child communication skills and provides a setting where family values are shared. Sharing meals provides a way to express family togetherness and affection and, in effect, nourishes the mind as well as the body. Family meals also serve to encourage family traditions and enhance cultural heritages.

Eating together used to be the rule and not the exception. My mother wouldn't let people begin eating until everyone was present at the table. But that was back when most moms didn't work outside the home. These days, the stay-at-home mom has become the exception rather than the rule. The challenges of life in the twenty-first century are taking their toll on the family in every way—spiritually, emotionally, and physically.

So, what shall we do? Shall we just go with the flow? Shall we just stand back and get used to it?

We can't go back to the good old days. Nevertheless, it is imperative that we wake up to what is going on now and take steps to mitigate the damages.

You may say, "But, Pastor O'Ffill, we're too busy to have family meals together." I once saw a sign that read, "If you are too busy to spend time with your children, you are busier than the devil."

Another natural preventative

Before I close this chapter on the family's health, I want to raise one more subject—one that gets less notice. No doubt you've heard of the eight natural remedies. It probably would be more accurate to call them eight natural preventatives. They are proper nutrition, exercise, water, sunlight, self-control, fresh air, rest, and trust in God. I think we should add another important component of health that scientific studies have confirmed as being a true healer of disease as well as a promoter of good health. This ninth remedy is humor. The impact of laughter on health was long ago documented in Scripture, "A merry heart does good, like medicine, but a broken spirit dries the bones" (Proverbs 17:22, NKJV.)

Some years ago, the author and editor Norman Cousins became ill with ankylosing spondylitis. (Even the name of the disease sounds painful!) He decided to use the positive emotions of faith, hope, laughter, and joy to counteract the effects of the stressful lifestyle that he believed had led to his illness. So, he treated his disease by watching comedies several times each day. His idea worked, and he recovered from the disease.

His experience aroused the curiosity of the medical community, and he was invited to teach at USCL Medical Center. Later, he coordinated the research efforts of scientists across the United States, and a summary of their findings was published in a book, *Head First: The Biology of Hope and the Healing Power of the Human Spirit.*

Drs. Lee Berk and Stanley Tan of Loma Linda University in California studied the effects of laughter on the immune system. The results of their studies were published in the September/October

1996 issue of *Humor and Health Journal.* These researchers discovered that laughter lowers blood pressure, reduces stress hormones, increases muscle flexion, and boosts immune function by raising levels of infection-fighting T-cells, a disease-fighting protein called Gamma-interferon, and B-cells, which produce disease-destroying antibodies. They reported that laughter also triggers the release of endorphins, the body's natural painkillers, and produces a general sense of well-being. Laughter has been so effective in helping people recover from illness that many hospitals have created humor rooms and humor carts. Still others have installed cable TV comedy channels, and some even employ clowns to make rounds each day.

Humor in the family

Laughter is not only beneficial to the physical health of individuals, but it can have a positive effect on the family as well. Laughing together connects us. It encourages understanding, facilitates communication, and builds a spirit of harmony.

In families with young children, humor can defuse what would otherwise be emotionally charged issues, and it encourages balanced disciplinary measures. Where humor exists, there is more likely to be a spirit of good will and cooperation.

In the family, laughter is a win/win because it

- helps us to bond with each other,
- increases the energy level,
- helps us to remember things better and can help us to solve problems,
- fights stress, and
- lowers blood pressure.

Laughter is even good exercise. Laughing one hundred times is equal to spending ten minutes on a rowing machine or fifteen minutes on a stationary bike.

Studies have revealed that children laugh an estimated three hundred to four hundred times a day, while adults laugh only about fifteen times a day. What would our homes be like if we adults laughed more? We shouldn't take ourselves so seriously. I'm not suggesting that we must laugh four hundred times a day, but I think many of us can do better than we do now.

We must be careful, however, that our sense of humor is not directed at other people. Rather, if other people are involved, we should laugh with them. This is important to model, because often the laughter among siblings has the sound of derision. Probably the healthiest kind of humor occurs when we laugh at ourselves.

My wife and I once assisted with an evangelistic meeting in the Russian Far East. The translator for the meetings shared with us how the communist regime intentionally repressed happiness in the children. He recounted that when, as a child, he would smile at school, the teacher would say, "Wipe that smile off your face!"

In the years that I worked in international relief and development, I saw some of the most pathetic aspects of the human condition. I remember visiting a refugee camp on the border of Thailand and Cambodia. The Khmer Rouge were fleeing the advancing Vietnamese army. When they arrived at the Thai border, they were starving, and hundreds were dying every day.

I will never forget walking through the refugee camp, which occupied no more than ten acres. Forty thousand people of all ages were living in this small area. As I walked through the misery, I noticed a complete absence of expression on the faces of the people. At funerals, the faces of the grieving family and of those who have come to pay their condolences show grief. But absolutely nothing registered on these faces.

As international aid agencies became involved, conditions in the camp slowly began to improve. The children were the first to reveal the human effects of these improvements. Whereas before they had been nearly catatonic, they now began to laugh and play again. The conditions were still pathetic, but hope had returned, and with it a smile. Where there is love and hope, there will be laughter.

If we are to be healthy physically, emotionally, and spiritually, we may need to lighten up in the home and not take ourselves so seriously. Again, I'm not suggesting that we laugh at the expense of each other but that we laugh together. As parents, we are responsible, as much as lies in our power, to provide an atmosphere that promotes good health in every aspect of our lives. A good sense of humor is free to all who will avail themselves of it and will go far to promote happiness and health in our homes.

Perhaps the question is not "McDonalds, what have you done to us?" Perhaps it is "What have we done to ourselves?" The next, and most important, question is "What steps are we now willing to take together to ensure that our homes are places where healthy habits are encouraged and modeled?" I hope you can think of some elements of a healthy lifestyle that you would like to bring back into your family—or, perhaps, implement for the first time. By the way, don't forget to smile!

I close this chapter with the words found in 3 John 2: "Beloved, I wish above all things that thou mayest prosper and be in health, even as thy soul prospereth."

Points to Ponder

1. Our heath is not our own business. We're responsible for our lifestyle both to God and to those who love us.
2. Fast foods have not only encouraged obesity in the family but also have undermined family mealtime.
3. We build family unity at the family dining table.
4. Watching television during mealtime can short-circuit the fellowship that we might otherwise have had.
5. A sense of humor can improve the health and well-being of the family, though we must be careful to laugh *with* each other, not *at* each other.

Homework Assignment

1. List three things you can do to make the atmosphere of your home more cheerful.
2. Make plans to eat together as a family at least once a day (without the television on).

---

1. See the American Academy of Child and Adolescent Psychiatry leaflet #79, "Facts for Families."

CHAPTER
16

Nobody's
Perfect

"Not as though I had already attained,
either were already perfect."—the apostle Paul

Some years ago I joined a book club. I decided to become a member when I received an ad offering me five books for only ninety-nine cents. But that wasn't all there was to it. The small print stated that I had to agree to buy at least four more books during the year, and twelve times a year, the club would send a notice announcing the book of the month and attaching a card. Unless I declined that month's offering within a certain time, the book would automatically be sent, and my account would be charged for the cost, plus postage and handling.

I could see myself forgetting to return the card and accumulating a pile of books that I didn't want, to say nothing of the money I would be spending. So, when I had received the five books for ninety-nine cents, I proceeded immediately to buy the required four books and then promptly canceled my membership. That way I didn't have to worry about returning the "don't send me the book this month" card. I haven't joined a book club since.

As the old saying goes, there's no such thing as a free lunch. Everything has a price, and we pay the price if we do nothing. The goal of the enemy of our souls is the destruction of our homes. If we simply sit back and do nothing, he will win by default. Unless we make and implement strategies to save our families, we will inevitably lose.

A young man once asked me what it would be like to live in the last days. I replied, "Like this." These are indeed the last days. Who would have dreamed it would be this way? Who could have imagined that one of the final objectives of the father of all terrorists would be the destruction of the family? But we should have known, because "divide and conquer" has always been his mantra.

In sports, there are players and there are spectators. The game of life differs. It has only players, no spectators. While we make every effort to insure our most valued possessions, somehow many of us leave our families unprotected. While many will go to court to secure their houses, land, cars, and monetary assets, many use the same legal system to dissolve their most important asset, their family. Suppose we could insure our marriages?

As I researched and wrote this book, I became personally convicted regarding the many times I have missed the mark over the years. But better late than never. True, nobody's perfect—but before it's too late, we must get serious. We can't go back and live our lives over again. And even with best intentions, we'll continue to miss the mark and fall short of the glory of God. But we must renew our resolve to press on toward the mark for the prize of the high-calling of God in Christ Jesus (Philippians 3:14).

Then what shall we do? How shall we begin?

Someone has said, "A less-than-perfect solution that works is infinitely better than a perfect solution that never happens." I was obliged to learn a foreign language when I was thirty-two years old. If you've never done that, let me inform you that to learn a new language as an adult, you must be willing to make a fool of yourself. Speaking takes practice, and you can't put off practicing until you speak fluently. This means that your first words are going to sound like those of a native speaker who is about eighteen months old. And so in our home life—while we can't go back and live our lives over again, we must go forward, even if in some cases we take only baby steps.

Sometimes when we compare our home life with the ideal and see how far we've missed the mark, we're almost overwhelmed. Some people even feel like giving up and accepting the status quo. They adopt an attitude that says "We've already made too many mistakes, and we can never meet the ideal, so what's the use trying?"

We could call another reaction "white-knuckling it." In this case, parents make a list a mile long of all the things that need to be done to bring their family up to speed. Then they take a deep breath, call a family council, and announce, "From now on . . ." If the first approach is underkill, the second is surely overkill. After a time, both, like water, will simply trickle down to their lowest level.

A simple proposal

So, where do we go from here? I hope that as you've read this book, you've begun to consider how your family can, by God's grace, implement some significant upgrades in your relationship with Him and with each other. If you haven't already made your own game plan, may I offer a simple proposal? We could call this proposal "The Christian Home in the Twenty-First Century." You don't need to have a Doctor of Divinity or a degree in biblical languages to understand it. This proposal suggests that a Christian home will have three main characteristics. I'm going to share them with you for your consideration and possible implementation.

1. The Christian home will be a place of prayer.

Members of the family should each have a private devotional life. Ideally, this devotional time will be in the morning. Of all the prayers we offer each day, it is the prayer in the morning that gives us focus for the day and puts us on the right track. Our spiritual lives improve exponentially when we spend time alone with God each day. Even young children can be taught to do this.

Christian parents must also conduct family worship. This worship shouldn't be long, and, if possible, each member of the family should have a specific part. It may include songs, stories, sharing of life's experiences, and, of course, prayer. Family worship is not a case of "one size fits all." It should be customized to the needs and situation of each home.

In addition, husbands and wives should pray together. I've discovered that families enjoy a great blessing when married couples follow this practice. My wife and I have always had the custom of family worship but not of praying together out loud, just the two of us. We've implemented this in our marriage, and I can recommend it highly to you. Once, during a prayer seminar that I was giving, a woman approached me. "Pastor," she said, "my husband and I prayed together for the first time last night. You should have heard what he said. I have so much respect for him now."

2. In a Christian home, the parents will take steps to counter the negative influence of television.

Typically, when a family decides to purchase a television, they plan to monitor the programming closely and even to censor the commercials. However, by a year later, they're watching virtually everything that comes on without realizing that anything has changed. It's safe to say that what the average Christian watches on television contravenes all that we pray the Holy Spirit will accomplish in our lives. Their television diet makes spiritual growth difficult if not impossible for them.

Researchers at the University of Washington examined the records of more than twenty-five hundred children. They found that 10 percent of them had attention disorders by age seven. The researchers then looked back at the children's television viewing habits at ages one and three. They found that television viewing increased the risk of having an attention problem by 9 percent for every hour of television watched a day.[1] Because of these findings, the American Academy of Pediatrics recommends that children younger than two not watch television at all.

Ideally, preschool children shouldn't watch TV either, and if they do, for only thirty minutes a day. Regardless of age or the programs being watched, no child should spend more than five hours a week in front of the television. In his book *A Family of Value*, John Rosemond suggests that TV doesn't keep children occupied; rather, it keeps them electronically drugged. The more time children spend watching TV, the more dependent they become on it.

3. In a Christian home, family members are intentionally kind to one another.

As I mentioned in an earlier chapter, most people are much kinder to those outside the home than they are to those whom they love and who love them. The premise of this book has been that, before the coming of Jesus, a message would arise that would turn the hearts of the parents to the children and of the children to the parents. This message is also embedded in Ephesians 4:31, 32: "Let all bitterness, and wrath, and anger, and clamour, and evil speaking, be put away from you, with all malice: And be ye kind one to another, tender-hearted, forgiving one another, even as God for Christ's sake hath forgiven you."

So you have it—three simple yet profound qualities of the Christian home in the end time: (1) it is a place of prayer, (2) the parents do something about TV, and (3) its members are kind to each other. How can we implement these qualities?

Have you ever made a New Year's resolution? Studies have shown that, generally, such resolutions last approximately five days. I'm a member of a health club. I've observed that at the beginning of a new year, the gym is crowded. When I pointed this out to one of the employees one year, he replied, "It's always this way after the first of the year. But don't worry—in a few weeks things will be back to normal."

Making changes in our lives not only takes extra effort, it also requires time, and we can't make time; we can only allocate it. In other words, when we want to bring something new into our lives, we must take something else out to make room for it. This is especially true of making time for personal devotions and family worship. Because each day has only twenty-four hours, putting first things first will mean that things of less importance will have to go. We will have no time for the things of God unless we reprioritize how we spend our time.

The ball is now in your court. It's in mine too. I'm praying that this book has been a blessing to you and that in the time remaining to us, the Holy Spirit will indeed turn our hearts to our children and our children's hearts to us. "For this cause I bow my knees unto the Father of our Lord Jesus Christ, of whom the whole family in heaven and earth is named, that he would grant you, according to the riches of his glory, to be strengthened with might by his Spirit" in our families (Ephesians 3:14-16).

Prayer of Commitment for Our Families

Dear Father of all families, we share the feelings of that great champion of the faith, the apostle Paul, when he said, "I count not myself to have apprehended: but this one thing I do, forgetting those things which are behind, and reaching forth unto those things which are before, I press toward the mark for the prize of the high calling of God in Christ Jesus."

Lord, thank You that, in spite of all that has gone before in our lives, You are a God of new beginnings. And so, right now we recommit our lives to You and commit to You our families. Father, we know not what course others may take, but by the grace of Jesus, Your Son, and by the indwelling of the Holy Spirit, we as individuals and as families will serve You. Amen.

---

1. See the March 2004 issue of *Pediatrics,* the journal of the American Academy of Pediatrics.

If you enjoyed this book, you'll enjoy these as well:

It Takes a Church
Gary L. Hopkins and Joyce W. Hopp. We all know the vital role parents have in transmitting values and faith to their children. But what role does the church family at large have? Gary and Joyce provide a practical and potentially revolutionary "Every-member's-guide" to keeping young people safe and saved.
0-8163-1904-9. Paperback.
US$8.99, Can$12.49.

We Can Keep Them in the Church
Compiled by Myrna Tetz with Gary Hopkins. In seven power-packed sections, church leaders like Ron Flowers, Willie Oliver, Noelene Johnsson, Aileen Andres Sox, Steve Case, Jose Rojas, and Karl Haffner share a wealth of specific actions that show members how to love our children so they won't leave.
0-8163-1998-7. Paperback.
US$14.99, Can$20.49.

Making Holidays Special
Celeste perrino Walker. Here's a creative collection of Adventist holiday traditions for you to enjoy and share, from New Year's Day to Christmas, and every celebration in between! In these pages you will find heartwarming stories, creative activities, delicious recipes, and lots of simple, heartfelt ways to show your own loved ones just how much you care.
0-8163-1956-1. Paperback.
US$4.97, Can$6.97.

Order from your ABC by calling **1-800-765-6955**, or get online and shop our virtual store at **www.AdventistBookCenter.com**.
- Read a chapter from your favorite book
- Order online
- Sign up for email notices on new products

Prices are subject to change.